Educational Accountability Reform in Norway

Lasse Skogvold Isaksen

Educational Accountability Reform in Norway

Education Policy as Imitation

PETER LANG

Bibliographic Information published by the Deutsche Nationalbibliothek

The Deutsche Nationalbibliothek lists this publication in the Deutsche Nationalbibliografie; detailed bibliographic data is available in the internet at http://dnb.d-nb.de.

Library of Congress Cataloging-in-Publication Data
A CIP catalog record for this book has been applied for at the Library of Congress.

Cover image: © BillionPhotos.com / Fotolia.com

ISBN 978-3-631-72845-1 (Print) · E-ISBN 978-3-631-72916-8 (E-PDF)
E-ISBN 978-3-631-72917-5 (EPUB) · E-ISBN 978-3-631-72918-2 (MOBI)
DOI 10.3726/b11476

© Peter Lang GmbH
Internationaler Verlag der Wissenschaften
Berlin 2018
All rights reserved.

Peter Lang – Berlin · Bern · Bruxelles · New York ·
Oxford · Warszawa · Wien

This publication has been peer reviewed.

www.peterlang.com

Abstract

This study explores the Norwegian educational accountability reform from 2001 to 2009 from an international comparative perspective. The reform can be seen as the Norwegian response to results from the Programme for International Student Assessment (PISA). The PISA results that were published in 2001 challenged the broadly held "first-class ticket" view of the national education system. Norway went from being more or less disconnected from international educational accountability policy to rapidly adapting to the international discourse and trends. One of the main assumptions behind the study is that the adoption of an international education policy need not produce the same policy (output) and results (outcome) in different national contexts. This study analyzes national education policy in the age of globalization as a result of an adjustment and transformation of international education policy and trends. The study asks how the national level in Norway, seen in the light of core political documents, understood international policy and transferred this to the Norwegian context. One of the main findings is that the international educational accountability policy was transformed in a manner in Norway that discarded the core rationale behind the policy.

Table of Contents

Part III. Educational Accountability Reform in Norway

1. Introduction

This book deals with the Norwegian educational accountability reform from 2001 to 2009. The aim of the study is to explore how an international educational policy, in this case an accountability policy, was transformed when implemented in a new national context. The Norwegian accountability reform has to be considered as a special case, not because of its failure or success, but because of the degree of transformation. It appears that Norway adopted and implemented a policy recommended by most international organizations, i.e. the Organization for Economic Co-operation and Development (OECD) the World Bank, United Nations (UN), European Union (EU), etc., but in reality developed a quasi-accountability system that more or less rejected the core political ideas and beliefs behind the policy. The paradox of global education policy is outlined by showing how a state implemented a recommended policy, but at the same time tuned and adjusted the policy and tools in a manner that discarded the core rationale.

A central issue in comparative education research is convergence in cross-national education policy. The two major questions here are *why* convergence has occurred and *if* the policies adopted are actually similar. Most studies in the field of comparative education have emphasized questions related to *why the policy is adopted*. In the eighties and nineties, comparative researchers more or less competed in efforts to show how neo-liberal ideology or new public management impacted their countries, and used this as an explanation of why accountability policies were emergent at national level. This convergence in policy was linked to a pronounced shift towards globalization. At the same time, some research set out to question whether national policies were indeed similar and so to an extent modified the idea of cross-national convergence. Often inspired by new institutionalism, the studies looked at how domestic differences in international institutions and structure have transformed accountability policy (Stefan Thomas Hopmann, 2008). The studies highlighted divergence where convergence had been assumed.

The present study emphasizes divergence rather than convergence. A focus on divergence also provides an opportunity to explore a domestic policy from a comparative perspective. One question in this study is whether the adoption of an international policy or program actually produces the expected policy output and results at national level (Holzinger & Knill, 2005; Stefan Thomas Hopmann, 2008; Rosenmund, 2007).

Analyzing the experiment of importing and exporting in policy is a familiar exercise. Western countries have exported policy around the globe for centuries, often understood as giving a helping hand to the less fortunate. The failure or the many unintended outcomes of this export and import has been a recurring topic and the research has mostly focused on third-world countries' lack of capacity to implement a given Western policy. The Norwegian accountability reform copied in a sense many other attempts to transfer a highly sophisticated policy into a new context without the wherewithal to relate and adapt this policy to local challenges. In a review, it is possible to outline the transformation of the policy by analyzing the reform process to disclose how or if the policy was comprehended and put into action.

Education policy is often developed in international arenas and is assumed to be "downloaded" to a national context. International organizations promote education policy for their members and current national educational policy is often a product of a transformation process of global policy into a national context. Analyzing national educational policy accordingly requires an understanding of the origin of the international policy that is adopted and an understanding of the national context within which policy is transformed and implemented. Policy is not developed in an international vacuum, but is a result of a particular social and economic context. The comparative approach is used in this study by first exploring the policy that is imported, using this as a framework to explore how a national context may work as a filter. In using identified generic features of educational accountability policy, it is possible to analyze how this filtering affects the actual policy that is applied, and discuss possible explanations for differences and similarities.

The Norwegian education reforms that were initiated at the beginning of the century have to be understood as more than an accountability reform. The reforms entailed objectives and tools that were not limited to educational accountability reform; there was a structural reform, a content reform, a teacher education reform, a knowledge promotion reform, etc. It is not the aim of this study to describe and analyze the Norwegian reform as a whole, but to identify and analyze the policy elements that set out to make the education system more accountable. The accountability reform was closely connected to the development and implementation of the National Quality Assessment System (NQAS), a system for national student tests.

In this chapter, the study is framed and linked to the research fields of comparative education, educational accountability research, and education policy research. The research questions are outlined and the comparative method and design are presented.

1.1 The Case: The Norwegian Educational Accountability Reform 2001-2009

During the last decade, Norway has enrolled in the global machinery of educational accountability systems (Elstad, Hopmann, Langfeldt, & Achieving School Accountability in Practice, 2008; Isaksen, 2008; Langfeldt, 2011). Numerous local and national accountability systems have been established as tools to secure quality in the education system. The centerpiece for education policy debate in Norway has been, and still is, the *NQAS*, the aims associated with tests that belong in this system, and the effects of the increasing number of systems for monitoring the learning outcome.

The Programme for International Student Assessment (PISA) results administered a sharp shock to the traditional view of the unified schools system in Norway. This continued with a succession of low ratings in international tests after 2001, culminating in 2006 when Norway had the lowest score among the Nordic countries and was rated below Latvia, Estonia, and Lithuania. The social democratic Prime Minister Stoltenberg in his New Year television address saw the 2006 PISA report as a painful warning:

> In Norway we are used to being at the top of international rankings, but last month we got an international report that showed that Norwegian schools are far from the top, actually under the mean. It is a painful warning. The government has got the message and we will review the school reforms of recent years. Have we loosened up too much of the framework around instruction? Have we placed too much responsibility on the single student and parent? (The Annual New Year Speech 2006 by Prime Minister Jens Stoltenberg).

External accountability is an alien element in the Norwegian education tradition. Norway can therefore serve as a valuable case for exploring the characteristic features of the system: the expectations, scenarios, and purpose behind the policy. It is also interesting to see how a country that for decades resisted participation in international student achievement tests, where recommendations from international organizations have not been followed in practical policy, suddenly made a U-turn after the PISA "shock wave" at the beginning of the century.

The Norwegian school system has been characterized by an absence of external accountability systems and a decentralized steering model (OECD, 1987). External educational accountability systems encountered a school system where national control has been systematically absent and rejected, and where the professional community had a dominant political role in the steering and development of the school system (OECD, 1987).

The Norwegian accountability reform that was set in motion from 2001 to 2009 had roots in domestic political discourses as far back as the late eighties. The OECD conducted a national review of Norway in 1988 that pointed to a lack of accountability in the education system. Most education policy development after 1989 made reference to the OECD review and the necessity of a response to the non-accountability it had highlighted. From the review in 1989 until the PISA shock in 2001, discourse focused on questions around what and why. Again and again during the nineties it was proposed that Parliament should implement a national system for quality control, but Parliament again and again was not able to agree on such a system. The PISA shock in 2001 jump-started Norwegian accountability policy. The reform can be divided into three phases: *the political groundwork period, implementation*, and *subsequent revision*.

1.1.1 Political Groundwork 2001–2004

The first phase from 2001 to 2004 can be seen as a political groundwork period. The policy behind the accountability reform was developed, both in terms of problem formulation and scenarios, and strategies were established. The two main political processes were associated with a project, *School Knows Best*, and the work of a committee, the *Committee for Quality*. Both drew upon well-known education scenarios embedded in educational accountability policy.

In 2001, Conservative parties won the election and formed a Conservative coalition. The coalition started a broad modernization program for public services (Arbeids- og administrasjonsdepartementet, 2002). The Royal Norwegian Ministry of Education and Research was led by Kristin Clemet, a central political figure at the time. *School Knows Best* was the vehicle of modernization in education (Norge . Utdannings- og forskningsdepartementet & Skolen vet best, 2002, 2003; Ødelien & Jacobsen, 2003). In October 2001, the *Committee for Quality in Primary and Secondary Education in Norway* was appointed. The Committee submitted a partial report in the spring of 2002 (Søgnen & Kvalitetsutvalget, 2002) and its main report to the Minister of Education in June 2003 (Søgnen & Kvalitetsutvalget, 2003). The Committee played a central role in the development of the Norwegian educational accountability reform. In 2004, the Royal Norwegian Ministry of Education submitted the White Paper *Culture for Learning* (K. f. l. Norge . Utdannings- og forskningsdepartementet, 2004) to Parliament. *Culture for Learning* summarized the political groundwork phase of the educational accountability reform. The documents from the *School Knows Best* project, the two reports from the *Quality Committee*, and the White Paper *Culture for Learning* are to be considered as the political groundwork for the Norwegian accountability reform.[1]

1.1.2 The Implementation of the System 2004–2006

From 2004, accountability policy tools were developed and implemented. Central was the web portal, skoleporten.no, where results from the new NQAS were to be published. The development of the national tests and their implementation has been seen as a major political failure. The policy lost support during its implementation despite being supported by all political parties during negotiations in Parliament. National tests were boycotted from the start by students and teachers. The system was abandoned by the new Social Democrat-led coalition government that took office in 2005. Evaluation of the tests was devastating and revealed a lack of clarity and poor system quality.

1.1.3 Subsequent Revision 2006–2009

The new Social Democrat government changed policy. In the coalition agreement from 2005, the function and purpose of the national test system were described and the coalition partners agreed on continuing testing, but in a new form and with a new focus. In 2005, the new government decided to suspend national testing in order to revise the system. The policy shift is evident in the two White Papers: *And no one was left behind* (Norge . Kunnskapsdepartementet, 2006) and *Quality in School* (Norge . Kunnskapsdepartementet, 2008). The NQAS was revised and started up again in 2007.

1.2 Research Field

It is not possible to identify one clearly defined education research field related to the present study. The design of the study, which will be presented later in the chapter, aims to connect educational accountability policy to its social and historical origins, and then explore how a specific national filter has transformed

---

1   Two reports from the *School Knows Best* project were produced (Norge. Utdannings-og forskningsdepartementet & Skolen vet best, 2002, 2003). Two White Papers were submitted by the Quality Committee (Søgnen & Kvalitetsutvalget, 2003; Søgnen, Kvalitetsutvalget, & Utdannings- og forskningsdepartementet, 2002) and a Report to Stortinget was produced: *Culture for learning* (K. f. l. Norge. Utdannings- og forskningsdepartementet, 2004).

the policy. To be able to explore the transformation process at the national level, it is necessary to outline a theoretical framework for the policy, in our case the generic features of educational accountability policy. To do so, we have to analyze its origin and the social context where the policy was developed. The transformation process can't be disconnected from its context, in our case, Norway. So the Norwegian education quality discourse is outlined, being fundamental for an exploration of the transformation of the policy that was adopted. And then the transformation process is analyzed with reference to the political groundwork behind the reform.

The study contributes to, and is a part of, different fields and research traditions, and as a case study, it must draw on a variety of research that can be useful for throwing light on its topic. Three fields are especially relevant: *comparative education policy research*, *educational accountability research*, and *education policy research*.

1.2.1 Comparative Education Policy Research

The basis of comparative education research is the theory and methodology of comparative study (Koehl, 1977). Until the 1950s, research mainly dealt with philosophical and cultural differences in the origins of national educational systems (Adick, 2005; Martin Carnoy & Diana Rhoten, 2002), and the field of comparative education has traditionally viewed changes in the education system as a result of the development of new philosophies or theories by pedagogues. Comparative studies conducted in the 1960s and 1970s challenged this traditional approach. They incorporated social and economic changes as explanations for education reforms and differences. Currently, social and economic conditions are understood as driving forces behind education reforms (Arnove, 1980). Education reforms are today analyzed in connection with, and as results of, social and economic changes, especially in relation to the knowledge-based economy paradigm in which the education system is given a central role in promoting stability and economic growth (R. Dale, 2005). The effects of globalization and internationalization on the education system have become one of the main disciplines in the field of comparative education (Hopman, 2007; S. Hopmann, Gundem, & Universitetet i Oslo . Pedagogisk forskningsinstitutt, 1998; S. Hopmann & Kunzli, 1997; Stefan Thomas Hopmann, 2008; Midtsundstad & Hopmann, 2011; Rosenmund, 2000, 2007).

Traditional comparative education research is built on the assumption that different social, historical, political, and religious values have determined the didactical features of different national education systems. A national education system reflects its national context. The field has been strongly attached to the philosophy of education. In the classic *Comparative Education*, Isaac L. Kandel, a professor in the philosophy of education, set out in 1933 some of the future goals for the research field:

> Still another method would be to undertake comparative studies of the quality of education in different countries; this, too, may be possible in time, but not before the instruments of measurement have been made more perfect and reliable than they are at present or when aims of education in different countries are more nearly alike, or finally, when tests have been developed which can measure more accurately the results of education rather than of instruction in fundamentals of subject matter (Kandel, 1933).

The contemporary "industry" of international comparative student outcome research (Kamens & Benavot, 2011) is part of the comparative education research field, but international student outcome research largely ignores the contextual *accepting* that has been strongly connected to the field. The socio-cultural and historical backgrounds that are the bedrock in comparative education are often absent in student achievement comparative research. It is challenging to link the current international industry to the long tradition of comparative research when it isn't accompanied by reflection on socio-cultural contexts. The future goals that Kandel described in 1933 for the field related to comparing the quality of the different national education systems were probably not intended to be separate from the heart of his comparative education research: the cultural and historical context.

Comparative education research has, since the 1970s, discussed the effects of internationalization and globalization on national education policy. Roger Dale has identified two different perspectives to explain cross-national education policy development: a common world educational culture and a globally structured education agenda (R. Dale, 2000). The proponents of the world culture of education "argue that the development of national educational systems and curricular categories is to be explained by universal models of education, state, and society, rather than by distinctive national factors" (R. Dale, 2000). The globally structured agenda perspective understands cross-national education policy as the result of a "systematic set of unavoidable issues for nation states that is framed by their relation to globalization" (R. Dale, 2000). According to Dale, states respond or react to the policy agenda followed by globalization. A new form of supranational force affects national educational systems. How states respond is explained by features and characteristics related to the single state. Dale understands the agenda of globalization in the light of competition between states and the imperatives imposed by economic growth.

Little attention is given to how globalization creates a public expectation that services and products can be measured against international rather than national standards. There is not a domestic market that is satisfied with less. In the same way as national cancer treatment is connected to international development and quality standards, the education system is viewed in a comparative perspective. Supranational forces serve to develop a global standard and knowledge-driven development, which domestic organizations have to connect to.

The increasing degree of internationalization in education policy has driven the field of comparative education toward the study of convergence in cross-national policy. The main idea in the field of convergence in policy is to analyze the level or degree of similarity in policy between nations. The field deals with the "... tendency for policies to grow more alike, in terms of increasing similarity in structures, processes, and performances" (Drezner, 2001 p. 53). These developments accompany a trend toward scenarios in policy areas that are shared by societies worldwide (Meyer & Krücken, 2005). Two of the most prominent scholars in the field of convergence in policy, Holzinger and Knill (2005), make a distinction between "... similarity of policy outputs (the policies adopted by a government) and policy outcomes (the actual effects of a policy in terms of goal achievement)" (Holzinger & Knill, 2005). The notion that the same education policy does not seem to produce similarity in outcome has inspired some comparative education researchers to ask why this should be so (Crossley, 2000; R. Dale, 2000, 2005; Stefan Thomas Hopmann, 2008; Susan L. Robertson, 2005; Rosenmund, 2000, 2007). Different effects and outcomes in different contexts (S. Hopmann & Kunzli, 1997; Stefan Thomas Hopmann, 2008), and on the other hand dissimilar policies, can have the same outcome; i.e. the Western middle class seems to adjust to different education systems and the outcome seems to be the same independent of education system, program, or policy.

International organizations such as the OECD are promoters of convergence in education policy (Bieber & Martens, 2011; Jakobi & Martens, 2010; Morgan, 2006). The influence of international organizations on national education policy poses a challenge for comparative education research, that is, to describe and analyze how nation states convey a global education policy or system into the domestic scene (Mundy, 1998). The readiness of the ministries of education around the world to respond to international organizations' scenarios for schooling has been examined as a factor in the development of international education policy (R. Dale & Robertson, 2009; Susan L. Robertson, 2005; Robertson*, 2005). How well-defined international scenarios and policies are elucidated and applied in different nations, i.e. in different socio-cultural contexts, seems to be a central topic in the field of comparative education research. One example of this type of research was conducted by Stefan Hopmann in his article *No child left behind* from 2008. He describes the dissimilar outcomes of educational accountability policy in the United States (US), Germany, and Norway (Stefan Thomas Hopmann, 2008). Another study revealed different effects of education policy promoted by the OECD in Switzerland and the US (Bieber & Martens, 2011). Christoph Knill identified five different mechanisms that create cross-national policy convergence (Knill, 2005). The first is the similarity resulting from a common independent response to similar problems. It is the policy problem of a lack of quality in the education system, and the nations respond in similar ways and irrespective of any shared cross-national policy. The second mechanism that Knill suggests is the exploitation of an asymmetric relation related to political and economic power. Less powerful countries are forced by other countries or international organizations to adopt a certain policy. Power also has to be connected to capacity to comprehend the policy. The level of education policy tradition and reflection can create an asymmetric relation between states and international policy agencies. It is possible to elaborate this to include how different agents support certain political views inside another country. The third mechanism is policy convergence due to an obligation to follow international law and regulations that countries themselves have taken part in constructing and negotiating. A fourth mechanism is mutual adjustment driven by the market. In education, the changes in the structure of higher education in the EU are an example of how national systems have adjusted to each other to facilitate mobility among students. The fifth mechanism is simply the effect of developing transnational communication. In education policy, most of these mechanisms are in play at the same time. The five mechanisms Knill discusses can be seen basically as communication and information exchange, but what triggers convergence in policy is often emergent similarities in social and economic structure. The same problems and social structures unleash expectations that need not require a specifically national policy response; instead one can adapt to policies from abroad that are suited to the same types of social and economic structure.

This form of transnational governance discussed by policy convergence researchers should not be mistaken for an abdication from governance, but rather the opposite, i.e. the use of increasing regulation and new systems for governing (Djelic & Sahlin-Andersson, 2006; Morgan, 2006). This transformation changes the relation between the state and its education system (Amos, 2010), but in the sense of governing without government (Rosenau & Czempiel, 1992). Educational accountability policy and tools can be regarded as the materialization of this new relation between states and their education systems. The policy conveys clear expectations of output rather than a defined input.

In modern paradigms such as *world society* or *globalization*, social and economic contexts are seen as parallel or similar and the paradigms convey a belief that it is possible to develop a common policy that is suitable in all nations, since we all encounter the same social and economic contexts in global society. Such viewpoints may undermine cultural and historical traditions in single national states, constrain their influence upon the impact of global policy, or inhibit the implementation of particular policies.

This study is part of the field of comparative education research, but instead of comparing countries' or states' education systems, it analyzes and describes how an international education policy, in this case, a policy that was originally developed in an Anglo-American context and made transnational, is imported into a national context without any experiences or tradition that align with the policy. The policy originated in a certain social and economic context and then developed on the international scene as an export policy that was recommended and promoted around the globe.

1.2.2 Education Policy Research

It is difficult to distinguish between education policies and education theory. Education policy is often limited to issues of governance, i.e. systems to control and manage the education system. But policy also draws upon theories of education, i.e. the function of schooling, goals, content, etc. At the same time, it is difficult to envisage any education theory that is divorced from policy.

Policymaking can be considered a process of social learning (Hall, 1993; Heclo, 1974). In this sense, educational accountability policy is the result of a social learning process. The learning process generates more than new policy instruments; it also develops collective notions and beliefs that are embedded in the policy instruments. Education policy is a result of a process of encountering challenges and it is a learning process that also entails previous experiences. P.A. Hall differentiated between policy paradigms and policy instruments and settings (Hall, 1993). The latter are much more likely to change than the ideas and beliefs in a policy paradigm. In comparative education, much effort and research has been conducted to demonstrate cross-national convergence in respect of policy instruments, while less effort has been devoted to exploring any convergence in education policy beliefs. Policy instruments are, however, expressions of deep-rooted ideas and beliefs embedded in society.

Education policy research has mainly been engaged in questions related to power, i.e. who influences or determines the direction of education policy at the national and international level (Apple, 2000, 2001; Stephen J. Ball, 1998, 2000). This tradition of education policy research has pointed out how particular groups have the power to influence education policy; this is often related to how these groups have conveyed a certain ideology into the education system. Globalization is viewed in the critical tradition as a neo-liberal attack on the national education system. Education policy research has aimed to critically analyze how the ruling classes have influenced education policy. The method of critical education research has been to analyze policy development and implementation seen in the light of critical theory linked to left-wing ideology. Norwegian education policy research has been strongly influenced by critical theory that defined every possible social and economic context in a particular ideological flavor. In the same way as in the rational policy research tradition, critical theory sees political decisions as more or less rational choices made by a certain global elite. According to critical tradition, almost all international education policies that are conveyed by organizations such as the OECD and World Bank represent by their very nature a neo-liberal and/or marketization of the national education system. Adapting to policy developed inside these organizations is the same as adapting to neo-liberal ideology. The state has a minor role in the common critical education tradition. International education policy as conveyed by member organizations is only used to legitimate certain policies (Ulf P Lundgren, 2011). The international organization is viewed as an agent for a defined social elite group.

Education policy developed in international organizations has progressively become more relevant as the national level increasingly confronts the same problems, i.e. the decline of the Western economy, multicultural populations, knowledge-based economics, mistrust of social institutions, a lack of basic skills, problems in recruiting skilled teachers, etc.

School reform is traditionally viewed as a political effort, i.e. after a time, a new reform is due and is generally rolled out in three phases: political groundwork, implementation, and evaluation (Stefan Thomas Hopmann, 2003; Tyack & Cuban, 1995). This study concentrates on the political groundwork phase. Analyzing groundwork documentation may suggest some explanations of outcome, i.e. outcome understood as purpose and function (Earl, Nusche, Maxwell, & Shewbridge, 2011; Lie, Caspersen, & Björnsson, 2004; Seland, Vibe, & Hovdhaugen, 2013).

The education system has been a key institution for the nation state in Europe, grounding each new generation into the values perceived as embedded in the nation and people and legitimizing meritocracy through equal opportunities and access. Transformation of the relationship between the nation state and the education system is one of the main questions in modern theories of education governance (M. K. Granheim & Lundgren, 1990; Kogan, Granheim, & Lundgren, 1990; Ulf P. Lundgren, 1979; Ulf P Lundgren, 2011). Educational accountability systems materialize and strengthen some features of the transformation: from input to output, from central to local, from teacher communities to school organizations, from a wide subject content to narrower basic cultural competences, from a national level to an international level, etc.

European education policy is grounded on the state role to define the national and/or religious content. The state level has had a central role in negotiating between different and conflicting interests. The public education system in the US was grounded on values related to the development of the single individual and the US concept of democracy. In the time of globalization, the traditional task of the national state in Europe of defining national and religious values are a challenge. And to some degree, education policy in the US and Europe has grown similar and European education policy is targeting the quality of the development of the individual as a means to sustain stability. The role of the state level is more or less reduced in Europe in the same manner as the federal level in the US, i.e. to secure and communicate equal quality as a tool to secure equal opportunities regardless of social background.

1.2.3 Educational Accountability Research

It is impossible to define a clear educational accountability research field. A definition of educational accountability policy is often followed by an outline of an educational accountability system. Elmore, Abelmann & Fuhrman (1996) define the *new educational accountability policy* by referring to three practical features: "student achievement tests, results published at the school level, and some kind of sanctions related to weak scores" (R. F. Elmore, Abelmann, & Fuhrman, 1996). Elmore's description captures the essential features of contemporary cross-national educational accountability policy.

In the US context, the policy is a part of the field of education theory (Bobbitt, 1918a, 1941; Carnoy, Elmore, & Siskin, 2003; R. F. Elmore, 1997; R. F. Elmore et al., 1996; Lessinger & Tyler, 1971; Tyler, 1971) and history (J. H. Spring, 2005). Monitoring and assessment of instruction is a systemic feature of American curriculum tradition and research. This research tradition is accompanied by a strong belief in the link between students' performances in achievement tests and the quality of the school. This link is not found in the continental didactic tradition in the same way as in the curriculum theory tradition in the US.

Educational accountability research in the US has mostly focused on the effect and consequences of educational accountability at the district level (Amrein & Berliner, 2002; Berliner, 2005; R. Elmore, 2003; R. Elmore & Fuhrman, 2001; R. F. Elmore, 1996) and at the school level (John B Diamond, 2012; John B. Diamond, Spillane, & Northwestern Univ. Evanston IL. Inst. for Policy Research., 2002; Mintrop, 2003, 2004a, 2004b; Sadovnik, O'Day, Bohrnstedt, & Borman, 2013). Less research has been conducted to explore the political ideas and beliefs behind the policy. An exception is a work by Jal Mehta that has explored how the paradigm of a knowledge society has created a political demand for educational accountability policy in the US (Mehta, 2013a). Richard Elmore's work has emphasized the political expectations behind the policy and explored some of the ideas and beliefs that are involved.

There isn't any strong educational accountability research tradition in Europe. If research exists, it is linked to the view of educational accountability as part of New Public Management or as a neo-liberal colonization of the national education system (G. J. J. Biesta, 2004; Biesta, 2005). It is viewed as a vehicle of market forces that drive the education system. The dominant critical theory research tradition links accountability policy to its common and general critique of neo-liberal ideology (Gordon & Whitty, 1997; Olssen, 2006; Olssen, Codd, & O'Neill, 2004; Olssen* & Peters, 2005). There is little, if any, education research in the continental tradition on accountability that doesn't convey a critique of the system or link the policy to neo-liberal ideology. Neo-liberal ideology gives the state a role, in contrast to classic liberalism, in creating a market by providing preconditions for competition and choice (Olssen* & Peters, 2005). It is about giving the hidden hand, the market mechanisms, a helping hand (Gordon & Whitty, 1997). Educational accountability is viewed in the critical tradition as an instrument to provide a quasi-market in public services or to implement market forces in a hitherto market force-free system (Bartlett & Le Grand, 1993; Le Grand, 2001; Le Grand & University of Bristol . School for Advanced Urban Studdies, 1990). The marketization of the education system is one of the main targets for critical education theory (Giroux, 2005), and accountability is viewed as a tool in the marketization process. The research does not include any empirical studies that can confirm that accountability policy is creating a quasi-market in education or that states are introducing accountability as a tool for marketization of the education sector. The OECD has conducted a study on the use of different educational accountability test systems among 35 of their member countries (OECD,

2011). The study distinguishes between three types of educational accountability: regulatory, performance, and market accountability. The traditional input-based regulatory accountability is visible in all countries. All of the 35 countries have some kind of performance accountability, but market-based accountability is scarcely used in any of the 35 countries in the study.

> Market accountability, which refers to the competitive pressures on schools, varies considerably across countries. While most countries permit diverse forms of school choice, in practice, the proportion of students practicing choice is more limited. Student choice does not seem to be a part of the international education policy (OECD, 2011, p. 441).

Gert Biesta frames his critique in a description of an accountability culture (G. J. Biesta, 2004; Biesta, 2005). This culture is transforming the relation between parents and school, to consumer and provider. It is viewed as antidemocratic in its nature and as a depoliticization of relations between students/parents and teachers/schools. The critical theory position on accountability involves an understanding of schooling and education as an activity that earlier was a non-market arena, a place for exchange of public goods free from market forces, i.e. without a provider and a consumer or without a demand and provider. Neo-liberal ideology represents a marketization of a relationship that had been free from human choices and asymmetric power. Such critiques are often accompanied by an assumption of a previously strong relation of trust between professions and the public, and a sudden rise of mistrust of public services that is more or less constructed by a rational neo-liberal policy (O'Neill, 2002b). Accountability in this sense represents capitalism for neo-Marxist-inspired critical theory. Autonomy for the teaching profession is somehow supposed to act as a bulwark against the market forces, by virtue of an internalized responsibility in the professional community (G. J. J. Biesta, 2004). The quality and equal distribution of goods are assumed to be secured by actions that embody the *mores* and ethics developed in the professional community as a self-regulating force. External direction of the system only serves to disrupt the professional accountability that secures equal quality and equal distribution. Research has not supported these claims; we do not have empirical studies of the distribution of education as public goods that show equal distribution or studies that confirm an asymmetric relation of trust between the public and the profession.

Student achievement tests are linked in the continental tradition to an internal steering of the system, i.e. school-based development and information to the school bureaucracy. The democratic aspect of assessment systems is not reflected and no distinction is made between data-driven school-based development and accountability policy as a part of the democratic system (Dalin, 1982; Dalin &

Rust, 1983). Research has seen national tests as tools to inform teachers, not as information for the public (Altrichter & Merki, 2010). In the US context, it is expected that schools and teachers themselves acquire knowledge of their students' learning process and use common standardized tests to make comparisons. External tests in the US context are related to the demand for accountability.

In the US research tradition, there is a clear distinction between high-stake testing and general accountability policy. In the European context, the distinction is often overlooked. Accountability as transparency regarding the quality of education in, for example, basic skills, isn't a political conflict area, but rather, is high-stake testing related to sanctions and a relocation of jurisdiction to conduct schooling on the basis of results is a contentious political issue (Carnoy et al., 2003; R. F. Elmore, 2003). The effects of *high-stake* accountability policy is a core issue in current US research (Amrein & Berliner, 2002; Berliner, 2005). In Europe, this research is often understood as being critical of educational accountability policy, but it is a critique against the consequences of high-stake testing and not the democratic right to transparency.

1.3 Research Questions: Differences and Similarities

Political school reforms often echo the evolution of schooling and can act as a vantage point that enables us to analyze debates and arguments revealing the changes in reflection on the function of schooling. In the aftermath of a reform, the white papers, political debate, evaluation report, articles, etc. are left behind as sources for analyzing the progression of theory of schooling in a permanently changing context. Therefore, reforms give us rich material to interpret the evolution of the function of schooling in a historical and social context. Political reforms are often analyzed in the light of various changes in, for example, social structures, the labor market, or political ideology that is materialized in the need for new ways of solving never-ending problems, in this case, mass schooling.

The new educational accountability system is the centerpiece of political school reforms in Western countries and represents changes in the nature of schooling in hyper-complex societies (Stefan Thomas Hopmann, 2008). New educational accountability reforms challenge and transform fundamental didactic differences related to content, goals, function, etc. Educational accountability has to be viewed as a part of the changes in mass education in the knowledge society. The policy mirrors the demand for mass education in the knowledge society.

1.3.1 Educational Accountability as a Transnational Policy

Educational accountability became the centerpiece of international education policy in the epoch of the global paradigm of a knowledge society. To analyze the Norwegian accountability reform from an international perspective, it is necessary to review the generic ideas and beliefs behind educational accountability policy. The policy is constructed in a context and entails certain generic features and expectations. Educational accountability policy emerged as an international education policy in the 1980s, but has its roots in the development of mass education in the US from the beginning of the last century. The policy was developed in a particular social and economic context in the US and was exported as global education policy. The description of the development of the policy and its features is fundamental to an understanding of the transformation of policy in the Norwegian context.

The evolution of the policy has had different phases and historical contexts. There have been shifts in the way in which policy is viewed. Accountability as a policy tool in the Norwegian context is related to the emergence of the knowledge society paradigm and differs from educational accountability policy related to, for example, the social efficiency movement in the US at the beginning of the last century. Educational accountability policy is strongly related to the idea that basic cultural skills such as reading, writing, and math skills are understood as a fundament for further learning or learning to learn. One of the main aims of mass schooling is to secure the development of these skills.

What are the generic features of the educational accountability policy?

1.3.2 The Norwegian Output

The Norwegian accountability reform can be interpreted as the adoption of a transnational education policy. This study explores how the national level in Norway comprehended the policy and defined it in the Norwegian context. The main purpose is to explore similarities and differences between international policy and policy output in Norway. From 2001 to 2004, a Conservative coalition developed the framework for accountability policy reform and the social democratic coalition implemented the policy from 2005 to 2009. The study focuses on policy development conducted during the Conservative coalition.

White papers are important landmarks in Norway; they define a political consensus. The search for consensus can threaten coherence in the policies developed, and the fine-tuned mechanisms of educational accountability and the necessity of coherence, a "fit" between different components of policy, can be jeopardized by the traditional emphasis on consensus.

How was educational accountability policy outlined in the groundwork document from 2002 to 2004?

1.3.3 The Norwegian Outcome

A range of evaluation research was conducted during the reform, both by international organizations such as the OECD and by domestic agencies. Using international and national evaluation reports, we will analyze the accountability policy that was implemented by the social democratic coalition from 2005 to 2009. The outcome of accountability policy is analyzed through secondary sources and central policy documents submitted by the Social Democrat government. Outcome is not related to changes in the school system, but to how the system that was put into action was able to make schools responsible for output.

Since educational accountability policy has not been developed and evolved over time in Norway, there may have been a risk of it being disconnected from fundamental ideas that define such a policy. One of the features of the reform in Norway was that the tools and the structure that were implemented were much disputed. There were fundamental disagreements about function and purpose. So we have to ask questions about the function and purpose of the Norwegian accountability system as it was implemented.

1.4 Design and Method

To be able to explore how distinct national factors affect the output and outcome of cross-national policy, the study has to have a suitable design. Cross-national policy has to be defined and the national context has to be analyzed to show how cross-national policy has been influenced by this national setting. The national setting (R. Dale, 2000, 2005) is seen as a set of distinct national factors, which bear upon the output and outcome of policy (Holzinger & Knill, 2005; Knill, 2005). In the case of the Norwegian accountability reform, we ask whether the generic factors that construct the fundamental logic of the policy have been present in the national setting. The logic of a comparative method is to compare factors that explain phenomena. By comparing, it is possible to determine what factors can explain differences. Most research entails a comparative logic, i.e. one experiment is compared to another experiment and the outcome is explained by determining possible differences. In comparative education, it is possible to explain differences from, or similarities to, national cultural and historical factors.

This study is based on the epistemology and methodological tradition of hermeneutics. The wealth of sources that is available in the wake of education reforms – policy documents, research and evaluation reports, political discussions, submissions from remarks from non-parliamentary organizations, toolboxes, textbooks, etc. – provides a large body of text that can be used to interpret the purpose and ideology behind the reform, and the process linking problem definition and understanding to the outcome of a policy. Education policy can be differentiated by using texts, trajectories, and different tools (Stephen J Ball, 1993). Educational accountability policies involve all of these different elements, which are integrated in a complex pattern. Ball emphasizes the complexity of education policy, which makes it necessary to distinguish between different levels, sources, and elements and adjust the research method according to the perspective chosen and the aims of the study (Stephen J Ball, 1993).

A fundamental requirement in the hermeneutic tradition is awareness of the position of the analyzer or reader. From Schleiermacher to Gadamer, the interpretation of text in the hermeneutic tradition is seen in relation to the context in which the text is written (Gadamer, 1965, 1967; Silverman & Gadamer, 1991; Skirbekk & Heidegger, 1999). The hermeneutic circle describes what happens when we interpret texts and construct meaning from their content, and how we understand the purpose and the intention of the authors. Meaning is constructed through the process of interpretation regardless of whether we are aware of the process. The traditional technical-empirical method used to analyze educational policy documents has been criticized for its naive confidence in languages as "… a transparent vehicle for the transmission of information, thoughts and values"(Codd, 1988 p. 236). An alternative approach, according to Codd, is to analyze policy documents as "… texts contain divergent meanings, contradictions and structured omissions, so that different effects are produced on different readers. Thus, it is suggested that the analysis of policy documents could be construed as a form of textual deconstruction"(Codd, 1988p. 243). According to Codd, policy documents often conceal the ideology behind the policy and construct a false consensus. He suggests a deconstruction of the text to reveal the hidden course of action. The documents are constructed to appeal to different readers and have the effect that the majority can identify with the policy. Policy documents are an expression of political goals and intentions. Codd's approach can be embedded in the tradition of the hermeneutic method. Political texts are written in a particular context of decision-making with the objective of obtaining support for scenarios, policy instruments, and strategies. Issues that are not discussed in the text can be as important as what *is* discussed in the text. These reflections relating to analytical methods are essential in this study, since the quality of the outcome of policy depends on a clear political statement of the purpose of the system.

In the paradigm of lending and borrowing policy, the traditional method of studying social and political changes is challenged by the fact that a policy in action on the national level isn't determined to be traditionally evolved over time in a geographic, social, or cultural context, but is only accepted by, or is a response to, international policy on a national level. The policy that is adopted does not necessarily mirror the social or cultural context, but the response to the policy is influenced by the context. Martin Carnoy and Diana Rhoten formulate a core question for comparative education research in an article from 2002:

> To what degree does educational change represent regional, national, or local responses to global economic restructuring, and to what degree do these changes represent international agencies' intentions regarding these responses? (Martin Carnoy & Diana Rhoten, 2002, p. 45)

Education policy has to be explored as a response to international agencies and a new economic order but not as disconnected from social and economic changes on the local level. Policy is developed in international arenas and is presented as possible responses to global economic restructuring; in our context, it is the paradigm of the knowledge-based economy acting as a framework to describe the global economic restructuring, and possible responses are negotiated and recommended on the international level. The American comparative education researcher Nelly Stromquist (2000) argues that the "... diffusion of ideas concerning school 'efficiency', 'accountability', and 'quality control'—essentially Anglo-American constructs—is turning schools all over the world into poor copies of romanticized views of private firms" (Stromquist, 2000, p. 262). Her position is common; contemporary international education policy consists of ideas from the Anglo-American context – mostly neo-liberal and those implied for economic growth (Stephen J. Ball, 1998, 2000) – and is more or less forced on other countries. Comparative education research has been, in the last decade, an elevated question around the mechanisms of how nations are complying to international organizations' recommendations (Stephen J. Ball, 1998; E. L. Dale, 1975; R. Dale, 2000, 2005; R. Dale & Robertson, 2009; Rinne, Kallo, & Hokka, 2004; Stromquist, 2000). The research has taken a critical position toward international policy and little criticism has been raised around the nations' response – how they have understood and used the policy. Furthermore, little focus has been given to how similarities in social and economic changes make the response to, or adoption of, the policy possible.

Most human activities and ideas are transnational, but are organized and institutionalized on a national level. Education, religion, and democracy are almost universal phenomena that have been exported and imported, and spread and transformed in different contexts. Democracy as a transnational ideology also creates a range of different formal and informal institutions in different nations. Why the same human phenomena are featured so differently between states has been a core issue in comparative political science. Failure or success in establishing democracy has been explained in the cultural traditions (Almond & Verba, 1963), and how different states have organized welfare systems is explained by pointing at national norms and culture (Esping-Andersen, 1990; Esping- Andersen, 1989). Comparing the differences and similarities of human phenomena in dissimilar contexts can reveal possible explanations and shed light on how characteristics in a context shape differences and similarities. Comparing makes it possible to reflect on the causes of the differences and the effect of the characteristics on how the phenomena are conducted.

The case in the study is defined as the adoption of an international education policy in a new national setting. This means that we have to explore the policy that is adapted, in this case, educational accountability. It requires an understanding of the historical development of the policy and how the policy is elevated to a transnational policy. It makes it possible to use the comparative method to explore similarities and differences between the policy put into action in Norway and the international policy that was adopted. To explore the transformation process, it is important to outline a clear picture of the policy that was supposed to be implemented in Norway.

Policy documents are the core sources for exploring how the international policy was deduced in a new national context. Analyzing the education policy using political documents is a method to explore the reform. Educational accountability has some generic tools to create the accountability dynamic. Exploring how the tools were understood and used is essential for exploring how the policy was put into action.

The first research question will be dealt with using a systematic-analytic method using core theoretical work in the construction and evolvement of educational accountability policy. The history of the development of educational accountability is outlined by interpreting some of the main scholars representing the movement in the US context. Educational accountability policy became a cross-national policy in the knowledge economy and the nations at risk paradigm. The main purpose is to develop a conceptual and analytic framework as a tool to analyze the Norwegian reform. The second research question will be answered by analyzing central political documents behind the reform. The reform can be divided between the development phase from 2001 to 2005 and the second phase where the policy was put into action from 2005 to 2009. The generic features of accountability policy are used as a framework to analyze the reform. The third question is explored by identifying features of national accountability policy and exploring possible explanations for differences in the output and outcome of policy.

Part I.
Educational Accountability Policy

2. The Origin and Development of Educational Accountability

The development of educational accountability can be observed through three distinct stages/historical contexts: as *connected to the social efficiency movement at the beginning of the 20th century* (Bobbitt, 1918a, 1918b, 1924), *in the area of unequal opportunities in the sixties and seventies* (Lessinger, 1970, 1971; Lessinger & Sabine, 1973; Lessinger & Tyler, 1971; Tyler, 1971), and *in the age of globalization/knowledge society* (Drucker, 1969, 1993; R. F. Elmore, 1997; R. F. Elmore et al., 1996; R. F. Elmore & Center for Policy Research in Education., 1990; R. F. Elmore, Fuhrman, & Association for Supervision and Curriculum Development., 1994; R. F. Elmore, McLaughlin, National Institute of Education (U.S.), & Rand Corporation., 1988; Eric Alan Hanushek & Kimko, 2000; S. Hopmann, 1991; Stefan Thomas Hopmann, 2008; Mehta, 2013a, 2013b; United States. National Commission on Excellence in Education., 1983). These stages are characterized by different theoretical, functional, and ideological legitimations of educational accountability. In the framework of historical institutionalism (Thelen, 1999), educational accountability policy is viewed as an institutional development in a historical and social context.

The first two phases in the history of educational accountability are related to the US context. In the last phase, accountability in the area of globalization and the knowledge society, educational accountability policy was translated into different national education systems around the world. Driven by international organizations such as the OECD and the World Bank, educational accountability has been implemented as the fundamental instrument for school reforms in the international context (Stefan Thomas Hopmann, 2008; B. Levin, 1998).

Most nations did not participate in the first phases of the development of educational accountability, in either its theoretical or practical aspects. Most countries became involved in educational accountability development and its discourse in the last stage/phase related to globalization and the knowledge economy. In this chapter, we will explore some of the historical connections and issues in the field of curriculum studies and school theory that have informed educational accountability.

2.1 Educational Accountability and the Scientific Curriculum Tradition

Educational accountability theory emerged in the wake of the scientific efficiency movement in the US. Franklin Bobbitt connected the scientific management movement to education theory. His two books, *The Curriculum* (1918) and *How to Make a Curriculum* (1924), outline a theory of curriculum development based on key theoretical foundations from the scientific management movement. Bobbitt represented the social efficiency movement in the field of education and he built his education theory on ideas developed in an industrial context.

According to Bobbitt, the hub for all educational planning was learning goals, revealed through a scientific method of studying real-life activities and what competences they require. Schooling had to prepare individuals for "fifty years of adulthood, not for the twenty years of childhood and youth" (Bobbitt, 1924, p. 8). The output-centered or goal-oriented curriculum theory of Bobbitt was the foundation of his idea of an educational measurement system.

Bobbitt defined educational objectives as *functional* (schooling as preparation for adult life) and *foundational* (as a by-product of daily life). *Functional education* aimed to prepare children for life's duties and the school, as a social institution, was responsible for this functional education. According to Bobbitt, the purpose of schooling was to teach skills that were identified as crucial for undertaking a role as a productive adult citizen. The school theory behind Bobbitt's curriculum theory was that the end and the means of schooling were to prepare students for life. The objectives in this functional education concerned everyone, regardless of social background or future role in society. Bobbitt gave the social institution of school a unique responsibility and role in the upbringing of the new generation. In 1918, Bobbitt published his article *The Plan for Measuring Educational Efficiency in Bay City* (Bobbitt, 1918b). It presented a student outcome measuring system established in 1915 in Bay City, Michigan, by Superintendent Frank A. Gause. With monthly student achievement tests, the superintendent was able to monitor the development of learning outcomes in the different schools in the city all the way down to the individual teacher. Bobbitt believed that this system made it possible to compare learning quality between schools and teachers. According to him "... the logic of the present measuring movement in the educational field is simple and irresistible" (Bobbitt, 1918b). The role of school leaders was "the discovery and elimination of shortcomings and defects" (Bobbitt, 1918b). The educational measuring system from Bay City has many similarities to modern educational accountability systems: student achievement tests, comparison of schools and teachers, and sanctions described by Bobbitt as *elimination of shortcomings and defects.* The achievement test systems described by Bobbitt are not conducted to measure student skills for selection purposes, but rather, the point of them is to monitor the *quality of schools and teachers,* and steer the system by sanctions on output. The emphasis on the quality of students' learning outcomes related to the quality of schools and teachers in Bobbitt's writing, rather than on the sum of the abilities of the individual student, mirrors some of the main assumptions embedded in modern educational accountability theories (see Stark, 1998).

So one of the hallmarks of the scientific curriculum tradition was that student tests were conducted not as an exam for selection purposes, but to measure the quality of the school. The differences between the two assessment traditions emerged during the last century (Travers & Westbury, 1989). Current educational accountability policy is linked to the scientific curriculum tradition by the outcome tests used as measures of quality or effect, and the view of the single school organization as a production unit that can be held accountable for its performance, or lack of performance. The scientific curriculum tradition, inspired by scientific management theories, brought the *school as an organization* onto the scene as an object of study.

The influence of the scientific management movement has often been underestimated (Merkle, 1980). Taylor and his associates are often understood as merely management technicians, and have been neglected by scholars. Indeed, their approach has often been seen as a defunct approach to management. According to Merkle, scientific management entails an ideology and has influenced the modern understanding of states, industry, and entrepreneurs (Merkle, 1980). The principles outlined by Taylor in his article from 1911 involve an ideological foundation for his theories of management:

> It is no single element, but rather this whole combination, that constitutes scientific management, which may be summarized as:
> Science, not rule of thumb.
> Harmony, not discord.
> Cooperation, not individualism.
> Maximum output, in place of restricted output.
> The development of each man to his greatest efficiency and prosperity (Taylor, 1911).

Taylor emphasized how science would create harmony and replace the tyranny in the workplace. A neutral groundwork of science would determine the relation between capital and labor. His management system would clarify expectations of labor and create harmony. It was possible to maximize outcome by replacing the rule of thumb with science. This optimistic, and naïve, belief in controlling and managing organizations is to some degree adopted by Bobbitt. Despite later attacks on Taylorism as a dehumanizing and profit-driven ideology, it was in its original form a movement that promised harmony, greater output, cooperation, efficiency, and prosperity. According to Merkle, "… Taylorism represented a technical ideology more than a set of tools" (Merkle, 1980, p. 15). In its management ideology, it set out to regulate relations between labor, capital, consumers, etc. A view of society is embedded in its tools for managing and controlling production and the benefits of production. Taylorism emerged in a social and economic context of conflict between capital and labor. He aimed to eliminate conflict by appealing to the common interest in a scientific approach. This interest had to do with what different agents could expect from each other, i.e. what could be done during a work hour based on scientific studies of the work process.

Bobbitt's curriculum tools for controlling and managing the learning process can also be said to represent a technical ideology – an ideology that conveys belief that it is possible to control and maximize learning outcomes based on scientific knowledge about learning. It also lifted schooling up to be considered as learning for life – in a productive sense. And it affirmed that it was possible to identify what was worth learning for adult life, in particular during the productive part of life. Bobbitt didn't use the term "accountability", but his work has to be considered as the harbinger of the ideology of educational accountability theory and policy.

2.2 Educational Accountability in the Area of Equal Opportunities and Social Reform

Leon M. Lessinger is viewed as one of the founders and first advocates of modern educational accountability (Bunda, 1979). His book *Every Kid a Winner: Accountability in Education*, published in 1970, is seen as an important milestone of the first "accountability movement" in the US. The poor quality of education for the underprivileged was the main motivation and a reaction to the socially deterministic approach of the Coleman report, which implied that schools didn't matter. *Every Kid a Winner* presented an optimistic view of what school could accomplish despite family background. What could be achieved only depended on how schools were run; they had to be based on knowledge and incentives for improvement.

Lessinger outlines theoretical expectations about student test-based accountability systems (Lessinger, 1970). The agenda of the accountability movement in the late 1970s in the US was to restore power to the professional educator, as a reaction to the community schools movement that had its focus on local control (J. H. Spring, 2005). Lessinger compared the perspective of local control over schools to local control over surgical treatment. The foundation for Lessinger's accountability approach was that schools had to be managed and governed by theory and practice based on research and development (R&D), a system that was pioneered by the American industry (Lessinger, 1970). According to Lessinger, a system of educational experts, called *school engineers*, should assume control over school management. The theory was inspired by the philosophy behind modern commercial management: schooling had to be outsourced to the best bidders or best school engineers.

An educational accountability system was, in Lessinger's work, part of what he described as an "educational engineering" process. In his article *Educational Engineering: Managing Change to Secure Stipulated Results for Disadvantaged Children* (1971), he abstracts the different stages in an educational engineering process and how these can secure the best practice in schools. At the core of accountability, in the framework of educational engineering, is the publication of school results based on student achievement tests at the school level. It is a key principle in the educational engineering process outlined by Lessinger that the public is given an insight into learning outcomes at the school level. In Lessinger's article of 1971 in *The Journal of Negro Education*, he argues that educational engineering challenges "… the traditional practice of withholding all but the most general information on educational accomplishment" (Lessinger, 1971, p. 47).

Educational engineering, as described by Lessinger, starts with the assumption that every child can succeed in school. The first educational accountability movement conveyed optimistic expectations about what schools could accomplish within a framework of accountability. An adequate technology of instruction and competent teachers would guarantee the results. In his description of an educational engineering process, the education expert had a central role in the Research & Development driven steering system.

In 1971, Leon M. Lessinger and Ralph W. Tyler edited the anthology *Accountability in Education* where a broader political understanding of educational accountability was presented (Lessinger & Tyler, 1971). Tyler's first lines in his article in 1971 give an insight into accountability in education at the beginning of the 1970s:

> Accountability has become a major subject of education discussions and a focus of sharp controversies. Ten years ago, the word rarely appeared in educational publications and was not mentioned on the programs of educational organizations. The sudden emergence of the term as applied to the process and outcome of education rather than to use of public funds deserves an explanation (Tyler, 1971, p. 1).

The work of Lessinger and Tyler was directed at challenges posed by the situation in inner-city schools and the situation of disadvantaged children in these environments. Research had confirmed the correlation between socio-economic status (SES) and educational opportunities (James S. Coleman, National Center for Educational Statistics, & Forente stater . Department of Health Education and Welfare, 1966).

Federal education policy in the US makes states accountable for their provision of equal opportunity to students from low-income families, often understood as a democratic right (Sadovnik et al., 2013). Equal opportunities are related to the quality of education and instruction given to the students rather than the quality of the student. Federal education policy in the US is more or less restricted to accountability policy, and in the act of 1965, it was already enshrined in law that the US would not develop a national curriculum (Bailey & Mosher, 1968). Education policy at the federal level wasn't an input policy. It was restricted to securing education opportunities for all by means of an output-based steering policy.

One of the better-known opponents of the Coleman report, Henry Levin, attacked the statistical methods used in the study. In his article of 1968, Levin and his co-writer Bowles concluded that it wasn't possible to determine school outcomes based on family background in the way that the Coleman study had done (Bowles & Levin, 1968). Behind this criticism was a strong belief that the quality of schools affected outcome. Schools were able to make a difference. In the 1960s and 1970s, Levin developed a theoretical framework for educational accountability. He identified four distinct perspectives for educational accountability, seen as *performance reporting, as a technical process, as a political process,* and *as an institutional process* (Goodlad, 1977; H. M. Levin, 1974). Levin aimed to design an educational accountability system that embraced all these four approaches. His study summarized some of the early thinking on accountability in the education system and also demonstrated the unmanageable issues encountered in creating a distinct theoretical framework for accountability. Indeed, his four perspectives illustrate the never-ending discourse about the meaning and theories of educational accountability. His work gives a broad representation of the second phase in the development of educational accountability related to equal opportunities and to building a system to protect the public against poor quality in public services (Stefan Thomas Hopmann, 2008).

In 1971, Tyler described changes in the function of schooling that accountability requires: "The first of these is the definition of tasks expected from schools, and the second is the widespread belief that schools are not accomplishing the tasks that they are expected to perform" (Bobbitt, 1941, p. 75). The definition of the task assigned to the education system changes due to changes in the labor market. According to Tyler, the criteria for judging the quality of schools was changing and this opened the way for accountability; earlier the public accepted that the main task for schools was to identify the talented few and to bring the majority into useful work. The public accepted that most children had limited potential for education and were absorbed into the labor market, a market in need of unskilled manpower; without any personal or public regret, most students went directly from high school into the labor market. Tyler suggested that schools should no longer be judged on the criteria of their quality or effectiveness in sorting the students by identifying the few talented enough for further education, but on securing basic skills for every child. In the past, the public had no doubt that success in school was related to individual ability and capability to learn. Tyler sensed a change; schools are increasingly held accountable for educating all children, not simply for sorting among students. "The school has assumed new and essential tasks, and it must learn how to perform them effectively" (Tyler, 1971, p. 77). Tyler interpreted public demand for accountability as a reaction to changes in the *function of schooling* and the recognition that a considerable proportion of young people are failing to meet the standards in literacy that "... now are demanded for employment in civilian and military jobs" (Tyler, 1971, p. 76). Tyler's explanation of the rise of accountability corresponds with his position on curriculum theory.

The second phase of educational accountability is linked in the US context to equal educational opportunities (Sciara & Jantz, 1972). Accountability systems were introduced on the federal level as a tool to get the different states to secure educational opportunities for students from low-income families. Educational accountability, as described in the Education Act of 1965, isn't presented as an educational theory that is supposed to deliver a new curriculum aimed at answering core educational questions. It was limited to increasing the quality of schooling for the social classes that didn't have any advocates at the state level or to increasing the quality of education in general (Bailey & Mosher, 1968; Jeffrey, 1978; Sadovnik et al., 2013).

2.3 Educational Accountability in the Knowledge Economy Paradigm

In the progression of the knowledge-based economy, the education system is elevated to a role as the core institution for securing economic development. Mass education is no longer a project to discipline the public or to socialize new generations to an imaginary community. Mass education is viewed as the foundation for inclusion and a lack of education is viewed as a cause for social exclusion. Schooling is drifting away from nation building to building nations for competition in a globalized marked. In the knowledge-based society, schooling has become an instrument for securing economic growth. The OECD emphasizes that the importance of education "... will be the center of the knowledge-based economy, and learning the tool of individual and organizational advancement" (OECD, 1996, p. 14).

There are some similarities here to the Sputnik shock in the 1950s that unleashed a space race between the superpowers, or the Western states' concern about the decline of their global economic power in the 1980s. This concern has not been restricted to the education system, but has involved many sectors. Mass schooling was linked to how Western nations could maintain economic dominance in an era increasingly characterized by a knowledge-based economy. Educational accountability policy became transnational and was promoted by organizations such as the OECD and the World Bank. Some concerns first discussed by Bobbitt and Taylor have been reinforced: mass schooling is related to further education and participation in the labor market. Education is required for everyone who will participate in the labor market. Mass schooling is no longer a means to identify the talented few but instead to develop the potential of the masses. There are too few blue-collar jobs and cornerstone industries are relocated to low-cost countries. So the masses have to enroll into the knowledge-based labor market. The manifesto for this political realignment is the report *Nation at Risk: The Imperative for Educational Reform* produced by President Ronald Reagan's National Commission on Excellence in Education, appointed in 1981. Its publication in 1983 was a landmark event in modern Western educational history (United States. National Commission on Excellence in Education., 1983). Among other things, the report contributed to the ever-growing (and still present) sense that American and Western schools are failing, and it set off a wave of local, state, and federal reform efforts. The report starts with a clear statement:

> Our nation is at risk. Our once unchallenged preeminence in commerce, industry, science, and technological innovation is being overtaken by competitors throughout the world. This report is concerned with only one of the many causes and dimensions of the problem, but it is the one that undergirds American prosperity, security, and civility. We report to the American people that while we can take justifiable pride in what our schools and colleges have historically accomplished and contributed to the United States and the well-being of its people, the educational foundations of our society are presently being eroded by a rising tide of mediocrity that threatens our very future as a nation

and a people. What was unimaginable a generation ago has begun to occur--others are matching and surpassing our educational attainments (United States. National Commission on Excellence in Education., 1983).

The Commission considers the decline in quality in the education system as a threat to the nation and its people. Other nations are perceived as doing much better and the US is in danger of losing out in global competition. The globalization of the economy and the knowledge-based economy is depicted as a challenge for a nation that over the years had benefited from its natural resources and access to motivated human beings from all over the world.

> It is not just that the South Koreans recently built the world's most efficient steel mill, or that American machine tools, once the pride of the world, are being displaced by German products. It is also that these developments signify a redistribution of trained capability throughout the globe. Knowledge, learning, information, and skilled intelligence are the new raw materials of international commerce and are today spreading throughout the world as vigorously as miracle drugs, synthetic fertilizers, and blue jeans did earlier. If only to keep and improve on the slim competitive edge we still retain in world markets, we must dedicate ourselves to the reform of our educational system for the benefit of all--old and young alike, affluent and poor, majority and minority. Learning is the indispensable investment required for success in the "information age" we are entering (United States. National Commission on Excellence in Education., 1983).

The anxieties expressed in the *Nation at Risk* report were exported from the US to most Western countries. The view of society embodied in the report was, in essential aspects, like the conceptualization of a knowledge-based society, introduced by Bell ten years earlier (Bell, 1973). The raw material in the new economy is knowledge and the ability or capacity to learn.

A profound mistrust directed at the education system is a subtext throughout the report. A never-ending catalogue of failures is combined with a sense of urgency. The nation is at risk due to the education system. The report also draws a picture of an education system that is totally out of control. It initiated a national and international reform movement that had its origin in education policy rather than education theory. Doubt about the quality of the education system and a perception of pressing social and economic change due to the rise of the knowledge-based economy encouraged reformers in their advocacy of change in which the public would take control over an education system that didn't meet the needs defined by the new economic order. The *Nation at Risk* report had profound influence in all Western countries and can be considered as a starting point of the education policy reform movement.

The current educational reform movement began in the 1980s in reaction to perceived shortcomings in education and international competition in all sectors. This world-wide movement has led to expectations for greater accountability and an increase in monitoring and evaluation of schools and systems. The search for meaningful information to help improve education led organizations to develop and implement indicator systems (McEwen, 1995, p. 3).

The scenario of a knowledge-based economy or society plays an important role in the dissemination of educational accountability. The core argument for school reform in the *Nation at Risk* report is the scenario of globalization and the advent of a knowledge-based economy. A nation's education system exhibiting low quality jeopardizes economic growth in the new economic order. In 1995, the OECD published the report *Knowledge-based economy*. It summarizes the discourse around the knowledge-based economy up to the mid-1990s. According to the report, more than 50% of the gross domestic product (GDP) in the members' countries was based on knowledge-based production (OECD, 1996). Labor market development mirrored this trend: "It is skilled labor that is in highest demand in the OECD countries. The average unemployment rate for people with lower-secondary education is 10.5 per cent, falling to 3.8 per cent for those with university education" (OECD, 1996, p. 10). Some of the scenarios anticipated by Bell in the early 1970s were now manifest.

The link between the knowledge economy and educational accountability is reflected in the core role of the education system in the new economy. Shortcomings do not only produce inequality, but shortcomings in the education system can contribute to economic decline. Industry and the economic system cannot accommodate the uneducated, and exclusion from the education system leads to a marginalization process. The education system is elevated to become the gateway for inclusion in all other social systems and this gateway is most important for low-income families with a poor network in the labor market. The most disadvantaged seem to become even more disadvantaged under the new economic order (Luhmann, 1997). Failure in the education system means exclusion from the economic system. The intensive and accelerated focus on the reality that poor children are receiving poor education is no longer a question of equal opportunity to attain social mobility, but is related to the fact that the knowledge-based economy does not have the same integrational dynamic as the industrial economy. When substantial numbers of people are failing in school or are not able to benefit from the education system, they will not be able to join the labor force in industry, and they will jeopardize society's stability and economy. The education system isn't only a place to sort members of a new generation into different inclusion patterns or levels, but also to sort them into inclusion or exclusion.

In the US context, educational accountability policy is mostly legitimated by the need to identify low-quality schools for low-income families, and the federal-level role is to ensure that states have tools to intervene. But the policy has always had a component of measuring annual progress in every indicator for all schools.

3. International Educational Accountability: The Core Features

The research field of convergence in policy aims to analyze the *differences* and *similarities* in output (*what policy is put into action*) and outcome (*the result and consequence*) of international policy at a national level (Drezner, 2001; Holzinger & Knill, 2005). The perspective assumes the existence of a defined body of international or transnational policy. To analyze the Norwegian accountability reform, it is necessary to construct a conceptual framework that epitomizes educational accountability in an ideal form as a framework for exploring the differences and similarities between the Norwegian reform and policy at the international level. It is methodologically impossible to isolate and define a pure form of an international educational accountability policy. In this chapter, the main *scenarios, policy ideas,* and *policy instruments* that educational accountability is based on are outlined.

3.1 Convergence in Scenarios

In the globalization paradigm of education policy, societies are assumed to encounter similar challenges (Meyer & Krücken, 2005). Educational accountability entails a convergence of scenarios in educational systems that serves as a legitimation or mandate for the policy.

Shortcomings in national education systems related to output quality seem to be one of the commonly perceived challenges among most Western states. The assumption of a decline in quality of the education system fuels public anxiety about falling behind in global economic competitions. Most Western states seem to view their education system as inefficient and unable to meet the expected objectives, putting their nation at risk. The main educational scenarios embedded in the accountability policy are related to the new role and function of schooling in the knowledge-based society, and mistrust of the system as it stands.

3.1.1 Knowledge-Based Economy – Nation at Risk Scenario

Jal Mehta links the development of educational accountability policy in the US to the paradigm of the knowledge-based economy (Mehta, 2013b). He describes how a paradigm creates policy in the case of education. The knowledge-based economy paradigm is accompanied by increasing anxiety in Western states, and a fear of economic decline against a background of competition between the

West and Asia, and this plays a central role as an argument behind educational accountability (OECD, 2001a; United States. National Commission on Excellence in Education., 1983). Education as a foundation for economic growth is axiomatic within educational accountability policy logic.

Theodore Levitt introduced the concept of globalization as a way of thinking about economic change (Levitt, 1986). The concept is currently applied to all areas, not only economic, but also cultural, political, and social changes. Combined with the idea of a global economic order, based on competition between states, the scenario of the knowledge-based economy has fuelled the international production of education policy. The EU-Lisbon conference in 2000 set up the goal of turning Europe into ".... the most competitive and dynamic knowledge-based economy in the world." The main concern in the knowledge-based economy scenario is that economic growth is becoming more and more dependent on knowledge rather than resources (Bell, 1973). In the knowledge-based economic area, the Western countries are not able to compete on wages and resources and have to invest in knowledge to secure economic hegemony. The global flow of ideas and production forces all sectors to relate to the global production of new knowledge. A hospital, a computer factory, or a school is not able to serve a home market with products and services that are not based on the leading edge of the knowledge economy. The quality of a computer, like that of education, is measured in a global context.

In the foreword to the newest edition of *The coming of post-industrial society: a venture in social forecasting* from 1999, one of the founders of the concept of the knowledge economy, Daniel Bell, emphasizes some features of the US context. He refers to trends that are seen in the emergence of the knowledge society. Infrastructure in the industrial society was transportation, and in the post-industrial society, it is communication. Demand for unskilled and semi-skilled work continues to decline. Human capital is the essential feature in measuring the strength and economic power of a society. Education has, according to Bell, become the basis for social inclusion and mobility. Even entrepreneurs need to have a higher-education background.

Services and products have to be knowledge-based, and not built upon long-accumulated traditions of supply and demand. The dynamics of the knowledge economy require innovations that can transform and create a demand and new markets. The point is not to satisfy a market or demand, but to create markets by means of innovation. Taking part and competing in the innovation economy requires a highly skilled population that can develop new services and products, which themselves create a market. The risk of economic decline is obvious if schools fail to provide society with a new type of workforce or work culture.

In a knowledge society, the marginalization dynamic starts with the compulsory education system (OECD, 1996). The traditional industrial economy embodied robust integration dynamics for those young people who for whatever reasons were excluded from further education after compulsory schooling (Frønes, 2010; Frønes & Strømme, 2010). Unskilled work was in demand in the production-oriented industry. In a knowledge society, the lack of basic skills appears to lead to marginalization. A knowledge society embodies a strong marginalization dynamic for those who drop out of the education system. The main expectation directed at compulsory schooling is to respond to this scenario by ensuring that everyone is proficient in basic skills, which are a requirement for all further education and learning. The OECD sums up this scenario in *The well-being of nations: the role of human and social capital* (OECD, 2001a). Schooling is emerging as the only route to inclusion, and instruction in and development of basic skills is seen as the cornerstone of social, political, and economic inclusion in a knowledge society.

In the knowledge-based economy, access to natural resources and a low-cost workforce are no longer sufficient to obtain economic growth. Nations are forced to compete to create social, cultural, political, and economic conditions for human creativity. States have to attract and create human capital that is not only able to compete in present market conditions, but can also create new markets and demands. The risk of falling behind in the knowledge-driven economy lifts the education system to the top of the political agenda. Quality in the education system is assumed to determine national economic development. The demand for educational accountability is emerging as mass education is becoming more and more closely related to production and the economic system. The risk that nations and societies are not able to take part in the knowledge-based market fuels public demand for high quality and standards in the domestic education system.

3.1.2 Function of Schooling in the Knowledge Society

A common feature of the scenarios is the role of schooling in the knowledge society: from producing a disciplined workforce to securing individual capacity for learning. The quality of schooling does not reside in identifying the talented minority, but in the schools' ability to develop a core of competence for all – the capacity to learn. In a knowledge society, the status of schools as public institutions is no longer related to their ability to transmit a defined body of knowledge to the next generation, and discover those with most aptitude in absorbing that knowledge. The schools' role is to be an expert in the development of the new generation's skills and its ability *to learn*. Teachers' roles and status are no longer related to their transmission of a body of knowledge designed for a hyper-complex society, but to their skill in facilitating the development of generic skills for further learning in the hyper-complex society. Quality isn't linked to the *given* characteristics of the individual, but *is* related to the education system's ability to *develop* the characteristics of the individual.

The school becomes the main gateway for inclusion in society and the paradigm affirms the quality of schooling as the means to secure inclusion (Frønes & Strømme, 2010; Stefan Thomas Hopmann, 2008; OECD, 2001b; J. H. Spring, 2005). Failure in school, in a knowledge society, jeopardizes social inclusion.

Childhood has become an essential and critical phase for qualification and ultimately for social inclusion. Schooling, in a knowledge society, is understood as a central part of an unending process or lifelong education (OECD, 1996, 2001b). Learning is no longer limited to schooling or educational institutions, but most human activity and creation are rooted in the ability to learn. The traditional function of schooling is very much changed in a knowledge-based society (Stefan T Hopmann, 2013). Learning and knowledge production take place in all social systems in the new society, and the role of schooling is changing from being a unique system providing for the few to being a cornerstone in social inclusion for all (OECD, 2001a, 2001b).

The industrial society had a labor market that was able to integrate new generations based on work ethics and discipline. Basic cultural skills such as reading, math, and writing weren't an essential requirement for inclusion in the labor market. Mass schooling, in its origin, was not education for work, but rather a form of socialization for work. The new role of schooling in the knowledge society is to provide the basic requirements for all further inclusion, i.e. learning to learn. The back-to-basics approach is certainly often understood (or misunderstood) as a neo-liberal or conservative value-based policy, but it only mirrors the function of schooling in the knowledge society.

Schools have a central position in the knowledge economic society since they have an essential role for inclusion, serving everyone during the years that are crucial for cognitive development, for *learning to learn*. In his article *Globalization or World Society*, Niklas Luhmann describes the change from a stratified society to a modern society by studying the changes in the dynamics of inclusion and exclusion (Luhmann, 1997). In modern society, "… functional systems presuppose inclusion of all, but in fact, they exclude persons that do not meet their requirements" (Luhmann, 1997, p. 70). He describes how one exclusion often serves as a basis and explanation of other exclusions. Luhmann's reflections about world society predict two forms of integration: the negative integration of exclusion and the positive integration of inclusion. The paradoxes of inclusion in modern society force the education system to become the main arena for securing the requirements for inclusion in a knowledge-based economic society. Luhmann admittedly does not discuss modern society as a knowledge-based economy, but his theories of mass education outlined in his book *Problems of reflection in the education system* (Luhmann & Schorr, 1979) do identify some of the same characteristics dealt with in knowledge-based economy theories. Luhmann has described the evolution of schools in three separate historical stages that reflect the changes in the function of schooling related to his system theory (Luhmann & Schorr, 1979). The social system theory that is based on Luhmann's functional-structural analysis defined function as a reflection of evolution, as part of the social systems' differentiation process. In modern system theory, based on Luhmann, social systems do not reflect functions that are connected to maintaining society as a whole.[2] Luhmann describes how learning to learn is becoming the main orientation for the education system (Tenorth, 1994, 2004).

The school system is called upon to adjust to demands and needs imposed by the knowledge-based economic reality. That means that in the future the labor or production market will be a market that demands knowledge and knowledge production. The education system, which earlier was the privileged agent of knowledge distribution and production, has to articulate new functions in the knowledge society, related to the foundation of further learning and education.

Accountability policy reflects the narrower function of schooling in the knowledge society (Rothstein, 2004). In the knowledge society, discourses that concern quality in religious or cultural education are more or less absent. Discourses that address compulsory schooling reflect how the schools' main function is to develop basic cultural skills for further learning. Schooling as part of a

---

2   Luhmann's functional-structural theory differs from Parsons' structural functionalism. Pearson understood the function of socialization/education as the maintenance of the societal community and the existence of a grand purpose or goal.
The maintenance of a normative order requires that it be implemented in a variety of respects: there must be very considerable – even if often quite incomplete – compliance with the behavioral expectations established by the values and norms. The most basic condition of such compliance is the internalization of a society's values and norms by its members, for such socialization underlies the consensual basis of a societal community" (Parsons, 1966) p.14).

religious or national project, as a transmitter of national cultural values, seems to be less important in the knowledge society. The quality of the school and education system is restricted to educators' proficiency in developing basic skills and this quality can be measured. This makes it possible to conduct quality output control by testing skills in a more effective way than when school quality was related to all possible skills and beliefs related to religious and national values.

3.1.3 Erosion of Trust Scenario

Accountability systems are often understood as a materialization of public mistrust directed at teachers and schools. Increasingly, mistrust or lack of confidence directed at public services is understood as one of the forces behind the widespread establishment of accountability systems (Behn, 2001; G. J. Biesta, 2004; Bryk & Schneider, 2002; O'Neill, 2002b; Power, 2003, 2004). The hypothesis of a growing mistrust of public services carries an assumption that the public had trust at a certain time in history and that this trust has eroded. Establishing accountability systems is in this sense a sign of erosion of trust in society. The focus on quality in schooling by parents and politicians can be understood as mistrust, but can also be seen as being related to a perception that society and the individual are wholly dependent on the quality of schooling, a perception that fuels public anxiety about failure.

So increasing mistrust in public services since the beginning of the 1970s has been seen as one explanation for the rise of accountability policy. In 2002, the British philosopher Onora O'Neill presented a BBC talk that has become famous: *A Question of Trust*. The speech was later published (O'Neill, 2002b). O'Neill had been working for years in the bioethical field. The relation between trust and autonomy in the field of medicine has been one of the main topics in her work (O'Neill, 2002a). O'Neill represents Neo-Kantian philosophy in the field of ethics. She identifies a "crisis of trust" and asks rhetorically if accountability can heal mistrust in our society. It is politicians, professions, and public institutions that according to O'Neill have lost the public's trust. An increasing demand for transparency is a sign of this mistrust and she refers to the "audit explosion" in Western society with reference to the work of Michael Power (Power, 1994, 1997). O'Neill describes the new culture of accountability in medicine, education, and policing, sectors that are represented by powerful professions professions that have had a high degree of autonomy and their own internal systems for control. Rhetorically she asks, as a university professor, how universities are going to increase quality and at the same time fulfill a political goal by accepting 50 per cent of each cohort in universities. O'Neill represents a traditional critique of accountability systems from the vantage point of the established traditional professions such as physicians, university professors, and teachers.

The discourse about trust and mistrust makes the assumption that institutions and professions at one time enjoyed trust and that this trust has eroded. Little evidence supports such an assumption. Whatever level of trust prevailed may have depended on an uneducated public that had no other option than to rely on professions and institutions that were assigned to solve complex problems in society. Re-establishing an uneducated public will probably increase trust and faith in institutions and professions but is not a feasible option in any society. Retrospective views of trust and confidence invested in professions and institutions seem indeed to be somewhat utopian.

There is little evidence that the public had trust in public services. Trust could be confused with respect based on different power positions, but this should not be understood as the same as trust. The majority of the public were unable to question the work done by professionals and trust in this context might better be seen as an aspect of unequal positioning in a hierarchy. A better-educated public today can question the services provided by professions. The discourse around trust and mistrust is often used to counter arguments that attack public services. Re-establishing the old form of trust in public services is the same as re-establishing an asymmetrical relation between the public and the professions, a position that seems unfeasible in a knowledge society. Growing mistrust directed at public schools is aligned with the emergence of the knowledge-based society. More and more, people have the capacity to evaluate the quality of the education system.

The more symmetric relations between professionals and the public in the knowledge-based society have led to attempts to reconstruct communication between schools and their central stakeholders. Parents are becoming informed consumers of education services rather than objects for values and aims defined by educational institutions. The family has primarily been expected to provide for the healthy emotional development of their children. In the knowledge-based society, the family must also take responsibility for the cognitive development of its children (Frønes, 2010; Frønes & Strømme, 2010). Parents in Western countries are investing more and more time and resources in the cognitive development of their children. They do not entrust this task to schools and teachers without closely monitoring and evaluating progress or lack of progress. This demand for transparency is not necessarily a sign of mistrust, but can be understood as the consequence of a shared responsibility for the development of students between schools and parents. A genuine shared interest can be mistaken for mistrust.

3.1.4 Shortcomings in the Education System

Economists have often been advocates for accountability, with a focus upon a lack of output related to the scale of resources put into the system. Economists naturally emphasize and develop theories around how institutions or private companies can be more effective and maximize their output. They focus on how to create systems that make schools and hospitals more cost-effective, but offer few theories or solutions on how schools or hospitals can be improved. Economists have been criticized for leading public institutions to believe that keeping to the budget and acting in a way that maximizes budgetary discipline and accountability is their main concern, so that a narrow economic focus ignores the core function of the institution. Economic discipline is an essential means for public institutions to meet their goals, but does not define these goals.

Economists can accordingly explain economic factors related to output and show how economic systems can act as a steering instrument in the public sector, but they do not discover or invent new medicines or learning methods. Economists are in the front line when it comes to promoting accountability in the public sector. Accountability has tended to rely on economic approaches rather than political theories. Economists explicate and reinforce a prevailing mistrust of how public money is spent in public institutions. In the development of educational accountability, reflection around, and awareness of, quality differences between education systems and educational institutions is a driving force (Hirsch, St. John-Brooks, OECD, & Centre for Educational Research and Innovation, 1995). The single school is viewed as the main target for developing the system. Educational economists have pointed out that the increasing use of resources in schools doesn't seem to create better results (Eric Alan Hanushek & Kimko, 2000; Rattsø, 2001). The economist Ludger Wössmann has shown in his comparative studies that there is no correlation between the amount of resources expended and results obtained, using material from Third International Mathematics and Science Study (TIMSS). He explains the quality differences observed by features of the different education systems and not by the amount of resources deployed (Fuchs & Wossmann, 2003).

The *money is not enough* paradigm, which means that it's often not possible to solve a problem with a bigger budget, means that it's often not a question of input, but rather an issue of what policy can create conditions that are a prerequisite for success. It will be important too to take a closer look at policies that are unsuccessful.

3.2 Convergence in Policy Ideas

The fundamental political idea behind educational accountability is that schools have to be given autonomy to decide on processes and use of resources. In other words, schools know best how to conduct schooling, while politicians must only define and measure the expected outputs. In one of the most referred to and influential OECD reports, *Governance in Transition: Public Management Reforms in OECD Countries* from 1995 (OECD, 1995), the general recommendations for good public governance are accountability, transparency, and decentralization. The report recommends a change in the steering of the public sector away from an emphasis on input to an emphasis on outputs (Dent, Bagley, & O'Neill, 1999).

3.2.1 From Process to Product

One of the generic common features of the idea of convergence in international policy is the development of goal-oriented steering models in the public sector. The policy instruments can be viewed as an apparatus to decentralize responsibility for processes to the organization level and to direct the system only by defining the objectives that should govern the process. This transition is often described as if the public sector has not been oriented toward goals and as if new public management is transforming aimless public institutions. But this is a very simplified and rhetorical view; all theory in education reflects objectives. Transformation from process to product can be better seen as a struggle in which a legitimated right to define goals is what is at issue.

Shifting the emphasis in education from input reform to output control has often been understood as a product of disappointment or resignation. Many attempts to reform the education sector by content and regulation policy have been seen to fail (Tyack & Cuban, 1995). System-wide school reforms do not seem to change and develop the system (Eric A. Hanushek, 2003) and so the response is to attempt reform by means of decentralization and product control (Hirsch et al., 1995; OECD, 1998, 2011). The OECD described and approved such a policy as far back as 1987 in a review of the Norwegian education system in that year (OECD, 1987). They praised the decentralization policy that Norway had adopted, but at the same time wanted systems that could control and monitor the quality of what individual schools produced.

Large-scale education reform targets all schools and does not take account of the fact that some schools are doing well, when we examine their output, and are not in need of reform. Output steering should be targeted at changing institutions that don't meet those quality standards defined by the authorities. Schools will be governed according to expectations about how students are expected to perform at a certain level in school. These expectations are directed at all students regardless of social background and talent. The fact that some students don't perform at the expected level is attributable to the quality in the schools concerned. The output is defined in relation to expectations. The public do not differentiate between groups or social classes and an output-based policy embodies a more child-centered ideology where the needs of, and expectations directed at, the single student are articulated by the school and its teachers.

Accountability is by its nature an ideological framework. Someone has to be responsible for the product of a process that is impossible to control completely, and to steer regardless of context. Reducing political control of the actual process or shifting attention from input to output is the prerequisite for making particular actors or agents responsible for the output. Political input to increase quality in public institutions is, within this paradigm, limited to the provision of a particular level of resources that is required to facilitate the process.

The quasi-marketization of the public sector (Le Grand, 2001; Le Grand & University of Bristol . School for Advanced Urban Studdies, 1990; Lundahl, 2002; Nir, 2003; Walford, 1996; Weiss & Steinert, 1996) has been one device used to introduce competition between institutions. This market-based approach is built on an assumption that there is a lack of incitements to better performance quality; indeed, the lack of such motivational factors is seen as the main factor accounting for a decrease in quality.

So the main idea is that the political system should not interfere in how school organizations set up and conduct processes that can help to achieve objectives. When politicians do regulate the process or define its content, they will have to assume responsibility for the result of the process, for the product. More autonomy granted to the school makes the school accountable for its product.

3.2.2 From Professional Community to School Organization

Teacher professionalization has played a significant role in pedagogical theory. Central characteristics of professions such as accreditation, development of a knowledge base, etc. are seen as the key to improving the quality of schooling. In this tradition, the route to better quality is that of promoting the status, training, and working conditions of teachers, that is, in furthering the professionalization of teachers and teaching (Ingersoll, 1997). The rationale supporting this view is that improving the status of the teaching profession will lead to improvements in the motivation and commitment of teachers, which, in turn, will lead to improvements in their enactment of roles and tasks, which will ultimately lead to improvements in student outcomes. Seen in this way, professionalization that enhances school quality and leads to better results is a complex of issues that are internal to the profession and not accessible to others. It can of course be asserted that the professionalism of this traditional cast will inhibit the forms of transparency that are an essential component in accountability policy.

One of the main challenges for the education system in the knowledge-based society is the recruitment of teachers. As the labor market becomes more and more globalized, teacher education is still bound to the national level. Oil engineers can be imported from all over the world, but primary teachers have to be recruited from the home population. Previously it was the case that undesirable social structures could actually benefit recruitment to the teaching profession. In Western countries, teacher training was one of the few feasible academic pathways for women. At the beginning of the last century, 95% of the primary school teachers in Norway were women. The school system for many decades recruited from at best half of the adult population. At the same time, teacher training colleges were the only academic pathway for the economically underprivileged. Until the education revolution of the 1960s and 1970s, teacher training education was the pre-eminent academic education for young people from poor rural areas.

Social structures based on inequality no longer provide the Western school system with a highly competent and motivated workforce. Recruitment to teacher training in Western countries has declined since the Second World War. The education system as a possible academic career must nowadays compete with almost all sectors that demand a highly educated workforce. The advantage of being one of the few workplaces for the academically trained workforce no longer exists and the status and trust that teachers formerly enjoyed cannot be established on the same foundations as in the industrial society.

The conflict between the ideology of professionalism and external pressure or management tools (Evetts, 2009) is often interpreted as a discourse of mistrust, but can be understood as a conflict of interests. External control is increasingly challenging the power of professionals to define goals and to distribute public goods.

3.2.3 Transparency

Accountability is accompanied by an imperative of transparency. Accountability is established through transparency. The public is given insight into differences in school quality and this insight is supposed to create a market where parents are able to make rational decisions and choices (Chubb & Moe, 1990;

West, Noden, Edge, & David, 1998; West & Pennell, 2000). This creates a basis for collective mobilization aimed at achievement at an organizational level. Power has described the emergence of an audit society, where all sectors have to create a sense of quasi-accountability for their performance (Power, 1994, 1997). One of the fundamental hallmarks of educational accountability policy is a demand for transparency.

Within the framework of neo-liberal ideology, the state provides requisite conditions for a marketization of public services by means of transparency. In the framework adopted in critical theory, social injustices in the distribution of schooling as a public good are made transparent and the systematic low quality of schools that serve low-income families can become a political and social issue. Transparency, or the demand for transparency, can't be restricted to being only an issue of corporate governance of the public sector. It is also a matter of the disclosure of systematic social inequalities in access to education.

The demand for transparency is of course intimately related to, and in a sense entangled with, the mistrust directed at the system. Disclosure of shortcomings of the system is one of the main political ideas behind accountability, and transparency regarding the ranking of institutions according to set standards will always convey failure and success, winners and losers.

3.3 Convergence in Policy Instruments

The common features of international educational accountability policy are three devices: achievement tests of students at a certain level in the education system, presentation of the results and comparison at the school level, and sanctions aligned with the system (R. F. Elmore et al., 1996). Assessment of students does not aim to test the single student's capacity, but assesses the effect at the school level. School accountability tests will accordingly differ from diagnostic or pedagogical tests that aim to explore individual characteristics independently of learning performance. Accountability also entails expectations about decision-making based on the data that are collected. Education accountability tools set out to initiate or further a dynamic of development. It is the dynamic that is the underlying logic rather than the tools in themselves.

In an audit society, according to Power (Power, 1994, 1997), tools have to be created that make it possible to make schooling transparent. In the education sector, this requires tools that show whether students meet expectations. It is not to set up the public sector's normal market based on supply and demand. Students' achievement tests are regarded as a tool for auditing the school system, but they also define a core content that can be measured and assessed.

3.3.1 Student Achievement Tests

The core policy instrument for the new educational accountability system is its quality indicators. The tests aim to measure the school effect. Tests are designed to test learning outcome, not to diagnose learning abilities. They aim to disclose differences in quality between schools. Though the students have to do the test, it is the school that is being tested.

In a study of 35 OECD member countries, only five did not have a system to measure school effects at the primary level in 2009 (Faubert, 2009). The study only registered the national assessment and did not include any data on the use of assessment at the local and regional level. Austria reported no national assessment, but there was a range of assessments used at the school district level, for example in the school district of Vienna. The same is the case in Germany and Norway, where some school districts have developed additional assessments used to hold schools accountable. So the OECD report is limited to accountability systems at the national level and does not show how school districts have established their own systems that are connected to international accountability policy. National achievement assessments of students are used in primary schools rather than national examinations that are directed at the single student level. In upper secondary school, most countries use examination results as accountability data.

One core issue in educational accountability research is whether it actually is possible to measure school effects using student tests (Bauer, 2000). Tests are narrow when seen in relation to the breadth of school curriculum content and the students' ability to apply knowledge and skills is seldom revealed in student tests. Education quality indicators based on student tests have a long history in the Anglo-American countries and represent a complex research field concerned with the development of indicators that are able to monitor quality differences between schools and quality development over time (Murnane & Raizen, 1988). This research area is different from that concerned with the development of learning and diagnostic tests (McWalters & Cheek, 2000; Oakes, 1989; Ogawa, Collom, & California Educational Research Cooperative Riverside., 1998). Indicators that are tools within educational accountability policy have their own distinctive design.

3.3.2 Identifying Failing School Organizations

One of the core beliefs and ideas in educational accountability policy is that schools are able to make a difference when they are of high quality. Instead of implementing a system-wide reform, the accountability system sets out to identify schools that are underperforming and applies external pressure to mobilize the school as an organization for change.

In the traditional centrally governed school system in Norway, where the school organization's main purpose has been to facilitate the work of the individual teacher, given an assignment by the state government, the advent of an accountability system intruded in a strongly traditional school *ethos*, in which individual teachers themselves interpreted centrally formulated goals. The roles of school owners (the local authority) and school leaders within the accountability system were seen as a threat to the authority of the teaching profession community.

Differences between schools in student performances that are attributed to organizational quality factors will be likely to challenge a traditional pedagogical approach to schooling – an approach that has ensured the quality of learning outcome through values and ethics that were developed within the professional community rather than in relation to objectives defined in the organization. The autonomous teacher, more or less independently of political and organizational steering, has been seen as a Holy Grail in European reform pedagogy.

In the US, the NCLB act was seen as a centralization of the school system, but in the centralized Norwegian school system, accountability was viewed as a reform to accomplish decentralization (Hopmann, 2008). Later we will ask whether the reform in Norway served as a form of centralization within schools, that is, a shift from a system based on teacher discretion and autonomy toward steering direction at the organizational (i.e. school) level.

3.3.3 Autonomy

The logic of accountability requires that institutions have the authority to make decisions about processes that determine output (Bunda, 1979; Ladd, 1996; H. M. Levin, 1974; Tyler, 1971; Wagner, 1989). In an input-based steering of the school, results are explained by how the school is able to align with external regulation of these processes. The schools can argue that they have done everything that the external regulator required of them, and it will then be impossible to make them accountable for the results. To make someone accountable for output, they have to be given authority over the process that leads to the results. We cannot make anyone accountable for a process they do not have authority over.

So decentralization of decision-making is one of the core features of a new educational accountability policy. This thinking is reinforced by doubt about how state levels can govern processes inside schools (Tyack & Cuban, 1995). System-wide reforms are abandoned in favor of establishing the school organization as the unit that has to make core decisions about the process. This shift also reflects a fundamental belief that schools themselves can attain the quality of output required. Educational accountability does not support the notion of autonomous teachers, but rather schools as organizations that have to have the necessary freedom of action. Without this, schools cannot be held responsible for results.

Part II.
Educational Quality Discourse in Norway

4. Education Quality Discourse: Equal Opportunities and Equal Results 1945–1990

An inward-looking and exceptionalist frame of mind in both policy and academic circles has fostered a view of Scandinavian schools as being profoundly different from schools elsewhere:

> In the international work reported here we again and again discovered that in the Nordic countries we see the objectives of education in a different way to that used in other countries. Schooling is one of the many ways to better society. In school in the Nordic countries students not only learn about their subjects, they also learn about life in a modern society. Societies in the Nordic countries expect that citizens are active and take responsibility (Ekholm & Ploug Olsen, 1991, p. 149).

The self-confidence and the lack of insight in other cultures' education systems may stop Norwegian education policy from connecting to the international reflection of quality in education. To demand comparative studies between such different educational horizons didn't seem logical ... *no longer learning facts from faculties* (as out there), but ... *learning about life in the modern society* (as here at home). According to the Ekholm and Ploug Olsenwo scholars, the Nordic education system had moved away from what was considered to be the archaic schooling objectives that the school structures in the other countries mirrored.

Though this Scandinavian inward-looking way of thinking is not a main issue here, it should be noted that social scientists have pointed to egalitarian features of society, with perceived equal opportunities and equality of results (Grendstad, Selle, Bortne, & Strømsnes, 2006). This extends to education, with educational quality being seen as a matter of equal rights andd an equal right to success based on individual features and talent. The development after 1945 of a school structure that secured similar opportunities, independently of student results, was accompanied by a never-ending elaboration of education objectives in the national learning plan, ending in 1997 as a description of almost all human activities as goals (Aasen & Telhaug, 1999; Norge . Kirke- og undervisningsdepartementet, 1987; Sethne, 1953). This is a catalogue so all-embracing that it would seem very hard for the individual student or the school system to fail at all. This proliferation of aims can be traced all the way back to the 1936 national curriculum; indeed, there has been a lengthy epoch in which almost any result of schooling could be regarded as a satisfying result for the system. The creation of *equal opportunities* is linked to the development of school structure, and *equal results* are connected to the never-ending expansion of goals and function of schooling described in the national curricula. Education quality in the Norwegian school policy tradition is challenging to evaluate, since it is associated with such a complex pedagogical discourse about goals.

The OECD review of the Norwegian school system in 1974 noted that the abolition of testing was regarded in Norway as "one of the major achievements of Norwegian policy" (OECD, 1976, p. 86). Reintroducing testing and grades was considered a threat to the broad objectives of the national curriculum tradition. Testing favors objectives that are measurable and the broad goals of the Norwegian school system have not been possible to capture in testing (OECD, 1976).

So the unique combination of equal opportunities and equal results in the Norwegian egalitarian tradition has influenced the education policy tradition. Educational quality discourse in Norway since the Second World War has been related to *quality as structure, quality as decentralization, the professionals as guarantors of quality, and quality seen as curriculum quality.*

4.1 School Structure as Quality

Norwegian politicians have used the structure of foreign education systems such as those in the US, England, and central Europe as a nightmare scenario for education in a modern welfare state. It has been a common belief that Norway has a school system that most countries desire. The Norwegian Minister of Education proclaimed in 1975 that the nation had the best school system in the world. Twenty years later the claim seemed to exemplify a naïve belief in the quality of the national education system. It is important to underline that political and public discourse in the sixties and seventies didn't reflect on quality as a learning outcome. The quality of the school system was linked to the overall political goal – *a system that gave access for all* – i.e. structural quality. Quality inside schools, in respect of learning outcome, didn't appear as an issue in the Norwegian school debate before the late 1980s. When the Minister of Education in 1975, Bjartmar Eide, claimed that Norway had developed a school system that most states aspired to, he and the public at the time didn't reflect on quality as a learning outcome, but on the Nordic unified school system that gave access for all – everyone attending the same school regardless of their social background. In the primary and only indicator of quality for schooling at that time, Norway may have had the best system in the world with its unified school system that included everyone in the same classroom for nine years of compulsory local school.

The central political documents, or groundwork documents (Norge. Utdannings- og forskningsdepartementet & Skolen vet best, 2002, 2003; Søgnen & Kvalitetsutvalget, 2002, 2003), behind the accountability reform in Norway reveal that until then, around the year 2000, the political discourse around education quality had been first and foremost linked to structural quality. The development of the unified school system was seen as a foundation in the formation of the social democratic welfare state. Norwegian school history is often depicted as a political battle for access for everyone to the education system (Aasen, 1999; Aasen & Telhaug, 1999). Schooling is treated as a *social right* rather than a *democratic right* as it is in the US. While most central European countries assign students at a certain level to discrete levels and education systems, i.e. vocational or academic courses, the Norwegian unified school system is a 10-year system, and the students that choose vocational training in the higher secondary-level years can get access to higher education at university and access to public service professional education at university colleges as teachers, social workers, kindergarten teachers, health service professionals, etc. The tracing system in the US, the private school system in Great Britain, and the *two* school systems in central Europe are rooted in national tradition and history. The Norwegian education system was more or less created after the Second World War without any established and firm tradition to build upon.

The unified school system has formed the common perception and definition of schooling in Norway; everyone is in the same local school regardless of socio-economic background and abilities. It is the cornerstone of the public view of education. Even the definition of schooling in Norway is linked to the concept of the unified school (Østerud & Johnsen, 2003). Equal opportunities in education are not confined to access for all, but everyone has to attend the same local school. Any emphasis on quality differentiation at the school level would threaten the perception that schooling is based on a unique combination of equal opportunities and results.

The Coleman report conveyed an attitude that schools are not in a position, or do not have the capacity, to help students that come from low SES backgrounds in the same way as students from high SES (Bernstein, 1973; Bernstein & Centre for Educational Research and Innovation, 1975; James S. Coleman et al., 1966). School quality systems based on learning outcome will in this paradigm be meaningless; they will merely reflect the social background of the student population that the school is serving. Ranking schools will provide a ranking by social background variables, a result beyond the control of the single schools. Coleman himself changed his views after studying private Catholic schools. He saw the effect of schools' organization and developed an optimistic view of what students can accomplish regardless of their social background (James Samuel Coleman, Hoffer, & Kilgore, 1982; Kahlenberg, 2001). The Norwegian Coleman report (Hernes & Knudsen, 1976) was based on data from the Norwegian education system. The authors saw a dilemma in Norwegian school policy:

> One dilemma in education policy is that when the school system is more effective in identifying the intelligent students suited for higher education the school system is a bridge to a new class-divided society based on intelligence and not social background (Hernes & Knudsen, 1976, p. 54).

Intelligence and ability are understood as the explanation for social differentiation in a society where equal rights and opportunities to education are realized, the means to this end being the unified school system. Differences in quality at the school level as a factor in differentiation are not dealt with in the report. Effective schools are schools that are able to identify the intelligent students. Gudmund Hernes, one of the authors of the report, had a central role in education policy development in the Social Democrat Party in Norway and served as the Minster of Education in the 1990s. The school effect movement in the US (Edmonds, 1979) that emerged as a reaction to the deterministic view conveyed in the Coleman reports didn't have much influence in Norway, apart from the work of a few scholars (Dalin, 1982; Dalin & Rust, 1983). School effect research had little influence in the Norwegian context and the view of single schools in the Coleman reports and the Norwegian equivalent carried out by Hernes and Knudsen is still dominant in Norwegian education policy discourse.

Structural quality in Norway is linked both to the unified school system as a goal in itself and to a strong belief in the schools' ability to reveal talent rather than to develop skills and abilities. Quality differences in a comparative educational perspective are understood as the ability the system has to include everyone independently of results.

4.2 Decentralization as Quality

In the sixties and seventies, Norwegian reform pedagogics were constructed by a long tradition of decentralization and the idea of school was anchored in rural tradition and values (Kristvik, 1920; Sethne, 1953; Sethne & Killingstad, 1928), values that in the rest of Scandinavia and Europe are regarded as a part of a conservative tradition that idealized rural culture (Spranger, 1928, 1932). In Norway, the *local school movement* took a radical form and defined a reform pedagogics that had the obligation to act as an antidote to accelerated urbanization and centralization in Norwegian society. The discourse of school quality in the Norwegian reform pedagogic tradition was connected to the perceived discrepancy between local identity, tradition, and culture that the students belonged to, and

values in national schooling that led to alienation (entfremdung). Reform pedagogics in Norway were aligning with conflicts of interest between urban and
rural or centralization and decentralization, the free economic market was seen
as the main force behind urbanization, and left-wing politicians embraced the
local school movement as a part of their critical tradition. The school as nation
building, the nation being defined by central areas, was considered a threat to
local ideals and values (Hoëm, 1969, 1978). School content that was evolving
in the local ethos was considered by the reform movement to be a barrier to
central government and control, and promoted as a way to emancipate students
from dominant central/class and urban values (Hellesnes, 1975, 1976). So the
main perspective in the Norwegian reform movement has been that a centrally
defined national school content undermines local values and alienates students
from their own culture (Høgmo & Solstad, 1977; Solstad, 1984, 1988). Reform
pedagogics in Norway in the sixties and seventies, as opposed to the rest of Europe, were not strongly related to social class theories, but to a theory of local
schooling that viewed national education policies as an agent of urbanization
and centralization. A central belief was that rural schools, with national content,
educated young people out of their own communities and into metropolitan culture, so that the school acted as an agent for the central government's rationali-
zation (Solstad, 1965). The local school movement defined a pedagogics whose
objective was to build sustainable local communities. School was regarded as a
valuable antidote to free market forces, forces beyond local control, which created urbanization and centralization. The national curriculum from 1987 to 1997
reflected the main pedagogical principles that the local school movement had
defined and developed in the previous decades.

In both national curriculum discourse (Høgmo, Tiller, Solstad, & Lofotprosjektet, 1981; Tiller, 1975, 1979, 1980) and the history of education and school
theory (Edvardsen, 1977, 1984; Edvardsen & Universitetet i Tromsø, 1985), alienation was the main strand in critiques of schooling. There was a strong at-
tachment to nature in this local tradition, i.e. the rural culture, and economics
and life in general were viewed as an adjustment to nature, rather than being
segmented domains for professions. According to the local school movement,
national schooling didn't reflect this adjustment to nature. The Norwegian local
school movement embedded the ideas of critical pedagogics, of schooling as an
agent for change, and a Nordic Rousseau-like notion of alienation from nature.

The local school movement did not involve, as in the US, the local people, represented by local political institutions, as the source of authority for the school.
Local control was viewed as the local teachers' control over schooling. Teachers'

autonomy was continually strengthened after 1945 and, according to the national curriculum (national learning plan) of 1987 (Norge . Kirke- og undervisningsdepartementet, 1987), the teachers, as far as possible, were supposed to agree on how the school was using their resources. The professional community was given the capacity to self-govern, even extending to the use of resources at the school level. Some of the curriculum ideas are still a part of the Norwegian discourse. The new classroom as a room outside of school and into the local nature and tradition is still a vital part of the curriculum discourse (Tiller, 1975, 1979, 1980; Tiller & Tiller, 2002).

4.3 National Learning Plan as Quality

Norway has a tradition of national learning plans (national curricula) employed as the main device for steering the school system. The learning plan, in the Norwegian tradition, isn't just a plan or document that describes content, objectives, etc. (Aasen & Telhaug, 1999). It is a strongly ideological document that outlines a national pedagogical platform rather than just learning objectives.

In its general section goals for the school system, the national learning plan of 1997 describes a novel description of "the seven human beings", i.e. *the spiritual human being, the creative human being, the working human being, the liberally educated human being, the social human being, the environmentally aware human being, and the integrated human being.* The seven human beings almost add up to schooling as a religious statement, since all aspects of life are included, and schooling has a moral and ethical obligation to work toward the development of the seven noble human beings. Most, or all, views of or beliefs about schooling can be found in the learning plan. It is hard to find an activity or a goal that isn't described in the general section.

These internal contradictions in the national curriculum and the very wide-ranging aims it embodied were however associated with a desire for professional freedom for the individual teacher to interpret the education goals and content (Tangerud, 1980). National learning plans might seem to be a strong regulatory input device, but in the Norwegian context, the plans were the result of an undecided political consensus that ensured autonomy for teachers.

4.4 Professional Community as Quality

Reliance on a self-regulated professional collective is strongly embedded in the Nordic welfare state (Grimen, 2005). Quality in services is to be obtained by developing ethical and moral reflection inside the professional community. This position is bolstered by an input-oriented steering policy where the community itself is set to develop high standards of practice. Pedagogical discourse in Norway, situated primarily in teacher training colleges, can be understood as a part of the professional teacher community's ethical and moral reflection. Educational research in Norway is mostly constructed around questions that aim to support professionalization, with the autonomous teacher as the ideal. External steering and control are seen as disruptive to the evolution and professionalization of teaching and convey mistrust of teachers' ability to do their job. Teachers' loyalty in Norway has traditionally been directed at the profession and its ethics and values, rather than toward the school as an organization. In the US, researchers such as Apple and Hargreaves have represented this kind of professional orientation. Traditionally, teacher education was more or less a form of socialization to the teacher profession community. Quality was secured by means of morals and ethics within the professional community. The Norwegian school system displays a combination of decentralization yet weak school organization (Helgesen, 2000). School organization has more or less facilitated teachers' autonomy and the local school owner, the municipality, has not had any role beside that of providing resources. Individual teachers have had responsibility for implementing national learning plans in the classroom. The professional communities and teachers' organizations have been central in the development of the Norwegian school system, and teachers have had an understanding of a direct line between themselves and Parliament, which legitimizes the learning plan. School organizations have even been regarded as an obstacle to the mandate that the single teachers have had from the national parliament.

So national learning plans have been seen as the political arbiter of what should go on in the classroom and the political system has traditionally used the learning plans as a way to secure different political interests. The inherent lack of clarity in the kind of curricula provided has created a space for single teachers to operationalize learning aims by themselves. In the Norwegian educational research community, research that mostly has to be considered a part of the professional community's internal discourse has been presented as an asset to enhance teacher autonomy (Tangerud, 1980). National learning plans in Norway have amounted to a catalogue of expectations rather than a statement of aims for steering schooling (E. L. Dale, 1975, 1980, 1986; Hellesnes et al., 1975).

The local school movement did reflect on the task of the school organization in the sense of facilitating collaboration among autonomous teachers. The underlying assumption in research dealing with the culture of school has been that professional autonomy can be secured in a school organization (Berg, 1983,

1995). Different cultural features of school were outlined and the collective responsibility of the individual professional was underlined. The school culture approach didn't embed any evaluation or steering, but offered a tool for understanding teachers' collectives. School culture research had influence and momentum partly because it nurtured the strong Norwegian tradition of teacher autonomy (Berg, 1983).

5. Education Quality Discourse 1990–2001

> The question of where accountability for the school is located – who will answer for its performance and to whom – is hardly perceived as an issue in Norway as yet (OECD, 1989b, p. 17).

The 1988 OECD review of the Norwegian school system has been characterized as the catalyst and starting point for a national school accountability discourse (OECD, 1989b). All white papers regarding the evaluation and steering of the Norwegian education system that were submitted after 1988 make references to the report and its aftermath. A growing uncertainty about output quality was emergent in the late eighties and nineties. One of the main issues in the nineties was the distribution of roles and responsibility between different levels in the education bureaucracy: municipalities, the state (central authorities), locally elected representatives, etc. (Engeland, Roald, & Langfeldt, 2008; Roald, 2010). The report and the public discussion related to it are an interesting window into the education policy debate at that stage.

The emerging skepticism in the eighties that was highlighted by the OECD review was succeeded in the nineties by a seemingly unending series of political documents dealing with evaluation and quality (Telhaug, 1990, 1992). With hindsight, quality discussions in the nineties didn't manage to define a clear political position on school quality. The traditional quality discourse was challenged, but this didn't produce any concrete alternative policy. The Nordic exceptionalist approach was clearly evident in the documents and conveys the view that the quality embedded in the Norwegian education system is virtually impossible to measure. There was neither a public nor a political pressure for insight and transparency. And the quality discourse seems to have been an activity organized for scholars and teachers and their unions sitting on one side of the table and the education bureaucracy on the other, sometimes agreeing and other times disagreeing at the next crossroad. The respective positions were well established and the political level didn't seem to interfere more than necessary. Parliament didn't provide any clear mandate to the government during the nineties (Aasen & Telhaug, 1999; Kirke- utdannings- og forskningsdepartementet, 1991, 1992; Norge . Kirke- utdannings- og forskningsdepartementet, 1996; Norge. Kirke- utdannings- og forskningsdepartementet Mot rikare mål : om einskapsskolen, 1999; Telhaug, 1999).

5.1 Emerging Mistrust in the Eighties and Nineties

Still, during the late eighties and in the nineties, the Norwegian quality discourse was challenged by doubts about the outcome quality of the system. In the White Paper *Med viten og vilje* (Universitets- og høyskoleutvalget & Hernes, 1988), a central question was asked: "Do we get enough competence out of the nation's talent?" (Universitets- og høyskoleutvalget & Hernes, 1988). The committee was led by Gudmund Hernes, who had written the Norwegian Coleman report (Hernes & Knudsen, 1976; Thuen & Vaage, 2004) and later became the Minister of Education in the nineties. The Nation at Risk discourse in the US and United Kingdom (UK) influenced Norwegian education policy discourse (Telhaug, 1990, 1992). According to Telhaug, a distinct shift in education policy was evident in most political parties during the eighties. The political focus moved away from the traditional structural perspective related to access and toward an emphasis on learning outcome and content knowledge (Telhaug, 1990, 1992). According to Telhaug, the centerpiece of the Norwegian education policy, i.e. equality and equal access in the sixties and seventies, was replaced during the eighties by a clearer focus on the function of knowledge content learning. This reflected contemporary international trends (Fend, 1984; Telhaug, 1999). This retrenchment can be understood as a conservative modernization of the education system (Aasen, 1999; Aasen & Telhaug, 1999; Telhaug, 1992). Quality concerns began to focus on whether the school system was able to prepare for higher education and the labor market, and structural concerns and debate were less in evidence.

But there were few signs at that time of any movement toward tighter control or evaluation. The Conservative Party in the eighties was more concerned with what they perceived as a need for greater autonomy both at the school and school owner level (Telhaug, 1999), but reflection on steering and controlling the education system was absent. So nothing amounting to a move toward accountability can be detected in the documentary record, even though doubt about school results was growing. The educational community had its gaze still fixed upon the system rather than the school.

This slow emergence of accountability as an issue in Norwegian education has to of course be seen in a national context. Education was manifestly an important issue in the context of rapid modernization and the knowledge-based oil economy. In the seventies, knowledge and manpower often had to be imported from overseas, but the future of the national economy would depend on high-cost knowledge development. This may have led to a strong emphasis on higher education rather than a more comprehensive approach in which the importance of schooling and acquisition of basic skills was appreciated.

5.2 The OECD Review in 1987

The review of the Norwegian school system issued by the OECD in 1987 raised questions about the Norwegian school system that would be much discussed in the ensuing decades. The recommendations made by the OECD committee have played a central role and served as a reference point in subsequent discourse about steering and quality monitoring of the education system. The report focused upon and questioned the national learning plan tradition and decentralization that were the basis of the new national learning plan implemented in the mid-eighties, Mønsterplan (Pattern plan/Frameworkplan) (Undervisningsdepartementet, 1987).

> From a curriculum theory and an educational planning perspective the new Mønsterplan (national learning plan) promises the use of curricula as instruments for governing. At the same time it has consequences for the overall planning process and for evaluation of the school system. In particular it raises the question: how can national goals for the compulsory school system be guaranteed within the framework of the Mønsterplan? Our evaluation of the compulsory education system in Norway has been structured by this question. It explains our emphasis on the need to build up a central evaluation and information system (OECD, 1989b, p. 18).

The committee had defined a clear mandate or focus for their review. Uncertainty and doubt about the system was a subtext in the report. They made references to different stakeholders who felt that the system was unable to "... provide young people necessary basic skills in Norwegian and mathematics" (OECD, 1989b, p. 7).

> We received conflicting evidence about the standards of schooling in Norway. Evidence of anxiety about them in some quarters was manifest. The demand for Back to basics has a familiar ring; it was expressed by employers, by those receiving students in higher education, and by some pupils themselves. [...] The fact that there is such anxiety and concern should be enough to evoke action from the schools, from local authorities and from the Ministry (OECD, 1987, p. 21).

The reports required a response from Norwegian school authorities. The report underlined that "... local authorities sustain a role essentially concerned with control over resources and over jurisdictional matters" (OECD, 1987, p. 22). As described in the sixties and seventies, local schooling in Norway was a teacher collective responsibility and the role of the local political level was to provide resources. The local school's movement was in fact a teacher-led community school. The OECD proposed that the principal or school leadership should be given a more defined and stronger role. And that the local authorities, i.e. the municipals "... need also to incorporate educational leadership, and evaluation and monitoring of the progress of schools" (OECD, 1987, p. 22). The review confronted the core approach of the Norwegian reform pedagogic tradition that had accelerated in the sixties and seventies and had its origins in the 1920s with homestead learning (Kristvik, 1920; Sethne, 1917, 1953; Sethne & Killingstad, 1928). The local school wasn't a local politically controlled school, but a professional community-controlled school.

> We noted, but were unable to pursue, the proposal that school leadership patterns should be adjusted to allow teachers' collectives. This is a proposal which touches on deep questions of accountability of professionals in democratically led systems as against the right of teachers to develop their own values and work within them (OECD, 1987, p. 19).

The OECD was reviewing at a time that has to be considered the peak of the local school movement's influence. Most of the reform ideas that were developed during the sixties and seventies materialized in the new learning plan of 1987.

Teacher autonomy and teacher professionalism in Norway was closely linked to a didactic discourse. Teacher autonomy was reinforced by a theoretical adherence to professionalization (E. L. Dale, 1975, 1986; Hellesnes et al., 1975). The learning plan reforms that had already started at the beginning of the nineties were a sign that the plan of 1987 was out of date at the time it was introduced.

In 1986, the earmarked state funding of schools ended, and schools had to compete with other municipal services for their funding. The decentralized school system was established and the role of the state level was not clearly defined. The OECD emphasized the need to establish an evaluation system that could produce steering information for the political level.

The report was structured around the question of how national learning goals could be guaranteed in the framework of national learning plans. National learning plans have been the main tool for governing schools in Norway and the OECD was questioning the prevailing confidence in national curricula or learning plans as adequate tools for steering.

The last part of the OECD report, *Critical Perspective and Proposals*, summed up the main issues that the review committee had dealt with – most of all, the lack of insight into, and evaluation of, the education system: "In examining international data, we were surprised by the absence of material which could be useful to the Norwegian authorities for their own planning" (OECD, 1987, p. 53).

The OECD report didn't propose a national educational accountability system. This wasn't on the agenda in Europe in the eighties. Monitoring and evaluation, as recommended by the committee, were to be provided to meet the central level's need for steering information. Transparency for the public regarding quality at the school level wasn't an issue in the report. One of the main questions posed by the committee was: "Would it be advisable to revise the structure for collation and use of data, both quantitative and qualitative, for assessing and monitoring the progress of the system to assist all levels in their policy making?" (OECD, 1987, p. 53). Together with questions about evaluation and monitoring, the committee was skeptical about the new self-governing school project that was outlined in the new learning plan:

> The problems that remain are not so much of provision and structure as of generating degrees of independence and strong professionalism within the schools. The Mønsterplan paves the way for a stronger teacher contribution towards better running of the schools. This being so, society will increasingly believe that it is for teachers to maintain and advance the standards of education now that they have the freedom to do so (OECD, 1987, p. 54).

The self-regulated school, without any political or public insight, is called into question:

> As far as the schools are concerned we would hope that they will develop a strong practice of self-critique and self-evaluation and at the same time will be able to seek help from external evaluation (OECD, 1987, p. 54).

The self-evaluation-based steering system that was established in the eighties was aligned with the decentralized ideology and professionalization agenda. The freedom that the Mønsterplan gave to the teachers served professionalization seen as an end in itself.

In the aftermath of the OECD review in 1988, a national R&D program was established by the Ministry of Education and Research, called EMIL. EMIL was supposed to examine the international experience of national evaluation programs, and to develop a national system for evaluation in Norway. A 400-page anthology, *Education quality – to steer or not* (M. Granheim, Lundgren, & Tiller, 1990), which rejected all forms of national evaluation systems, was the outcome. This was symptomatic of the Norwegian accountability debate before the PISA shock in 2001 – a never-ending discussion around why, what, and how (Moe, 2010). At the time, there wasn't any political or public pressure to establish any accountability systems (Aasen, 1999; Aasen & Telhaug, 1999; Telhaug, 1999). EMIL didn't deliver any clear recommendations, and in retrospect it connected to the traditional Norwegian didactical discourse as we know it from the sixties and seventies. Ulf Lundgren, who was a member of the OECD review committee in 1987, was also a central member in the EMIL project. In the anthology of his article, he again raised some of the questions asked by the OECD committee(U. Lundgren, 1990).

Kai Eide, a central Norwegian educational economist, contributed in the EMIL project and his reflections on the relationship between professionalism and evaluation in the anthology were an interesting response to the challenges set forth by the OECD review. He argued that the strong and well-developed welfare state in Norway had also fostered professionalization. Professionals were entrusted with self-regulation, and were to resolve core questions relating to whether the professional community serves clients' interests or their own interests. This is perhaps the reason why external evaluation of professional services such as schooling has come onto the political agenda. When this happens, it provokes defensive attitudes among professionals and a vicious circle with entrenched and mutually reinforcing standpoints can ensue.

The pronounced professional freedom that was given to the teaching profession from the sixties to the eighties came under attack and was seen as a considerable obstacle to the development of external quality policy in the nineties and during the accountability reform phase at the beginning of the new century.

5.3 Intentions, but no Further – White Papers in the Nineties

It had become obvious that Norway lacked a system for monitoring quality. After the OECD review (OECD, 1989b), discussion about the lack of such a system had been a recurring issue in White Papers (Norge . Kirke- utdannings- og forskningsdepartementet, 1992, 1996, 1999). The main approach at that time was built on the school-based evaluation tradition outlined in the White Paper *Richer Goals* (Norge . Kirke- utdannings- og forskningsdepartementet, 1999). National and external evaluation related to student achievement tests had been rejected. School-based assessment, or professional community-based evaluation, was adopted as the overall approach in schools. *Skolebasert vurdering: en innføring* (Ålvik, 1991) was based on ideas derived from Stenhouse and Schon that emphasized teachers' rights and competences to assess their own practice.

A number of White Papers during the nineties discussed and proposed a national evaluation or quality-measuring system. Already in 1991, the Report to Stortinget nr. 37 (1990–91) *Om organisering og styring i utdanningssektoren* (About organizing and steering the education sector) (Kirke- utdannings- og forskningsdepartementet, 1991) had introduced *management by objectives* as the preferred method of steering the education system. The Report to Stortinget nr. 33 (1991–92) *Kunnskap og kyndighet: Om visse sider ved videregående opplæring* (Knowledge and Skills: About some issues regarding higher secondary school)

(Kirke- utdannings- og forskningsdepartementet, 1992) suggested the establishment of a national system to evaluate the extent to which students reached learning objectives in higher secondary schools (Roald, 2010). The system that was suggested was supposed to produce results at the school level.

In the mid-nineties, the Report to Stortinget nr. 47 *Om elevvurdering, skolebasert vurdering og nasjonalt vurderingssystem* (About student assessment, school-based evaluation and a national evaluation system) (Norge . Kirke- utdannings- og forskningsdepartementet, 1996) outlined a proposal for a national system for evaluation. Norway was at this stage close to responding to the challenges set out by the OECD.

But it became clear that when the proposals were negotiated in Parliament in the nineties, they didn't have political support. Discussion ended in a diffuse wrangle around the definition of quality. At the end of the nineties, the Report to Stortinget *Aiming for higher goals* concluded that there was no need for a national assessment system and this more or less shelved the recommendations given ten years earlier by the OECD. Ola Moe, who led the committee, characterized its deliberations as an endless dispute about definitions and premises.

The PISA shock in 2001 changed the political environment. In retrospect, the 1990s appears to have been a period of conflict about the distribution of power in the education system. Employers – municipalities – had, as before, little real power, while central authorities surrendered much of their power because decentralization strengthened the teaching profession's grip on what went on in schools.

Part III.
Educational Accountability
Reform in Norway

6. Political Groundwork Documents 2001–2005

The education policy documents that were developed and negotiated under the Conservative coalition government from 2001 to 2005 were the political groundwork documents for the accountability reform. When the social democratic government lost the election in 2001, the new Conservative coalition gained momentum for their internationally orientated education policy in the wake of the PISA shock. The Deputy Minister of Education (2001–2005) presented his view in an article in 2006. The school system that was assessed by PISA in 2001 was associated with social democratic ideology. The PISA results created a momentum for a traditional conservative *back to basics* education policy (Bergesen, 2006, p. 6).

Whatever the justification for such party political assertions, the principles and intentions behind the accountability reform were outlined in three political processes and their associated documents: *The Committee for Quality in Primary and Secondary Education in Norway* (Søgnen & Kvalitetsutvalget, 2002, 2003), *The School Knows Best* (Norge . Utdannings- og forskningsdepartementet & Skolen vet best, 2002, 2003), and *Culture for Learning* (K. f. l. Norge . Utdannings- og forskningsdepartementet, 2004). The Quality Committee submitted a preliminary report, a proposal for a national quality system *First class from first year* (Søgnen & Kvalitetsutvalget, 2002) in June 2002, and the main report *In the first division* (Søgnen & Kvalitetsutvalget, 2003) was submitted in June 2003. The modernization project, *School Knows Best*, which was facilitated and organized by the Ministry of Education, published two reports before the new Directorate of Education reformed the reports to act as domestic *education at glance* reports. The first of these was the White Paper *Culture for Learning* (Norge . Utdannings- og forskningsdepartementet, 2004) as negotiated in Parliament in 2004. The Report to Stortinget *Culture for Learning* served as a summary of the policies that were developed during the Conservative coalition government's time in office.

The different political processes were interlocked, not only in relation to the issues dealt with, but also by the same actors having central roles in the different processes. The political process as such is not our main concern here, but the documents have to be understood and interpreted as part of an overriding political process led by central actors in the Ministry of Education.

The policy groundwork documents will be presented in this chapter: first, the reports from *The School Knows Best* reports, then the two White Papers that were submitted by The Committee for Quality, and last the Report to Stortinget *Culture for learning*.

6.1 School Knows Best – The Reports

The *School Knows Best* was an internally organized project of the Ministry of Education and was linked to an overall national modernization program of the public sector. In a White Paper in the spring of 2002, the general objectives for the project were set out (Arbeids- og administrasjonsdepartementet, 2002). The first phase of the Ministry of Education project was labelled *Modernization of the compulsory school system* before the name was changed to *School Knows Best*. Two reports were published: one in 2002 and one in 2003. After 2003, the reports became a part of the annual report from the new Directorate of Education. It was intended to serve as an *education at glance* report at the national level.

Modernization of the public sector was one of the main aims for the new Conservative coalition government that took office in 2001. The *School Knows Best* project was divided into five subprojects. Subproject L was *The legal framework for schools*; its aim was to give the school owners, i.e. the municipals, a legal basis for steering their schools. Subproject F, *Finance*, aimed to establish a fiscal system that could enhance the quality and effective use of resources. Subproject K, *Quality*, aimed to establish tools for monitoring and developing quality. Subproject O, *Organization*, aimed to clarify roles and responsibilities for the different bureaucratic levels in the system. The overall objective was to organize school administration in such a way that the responsibility of the school owner could be defined in connection with quality, and the role of the state level was to control, supervise, conduct quality assessments, and coordinate development in the sector. Subproject I, *Information*, was concerned with the need for internal and external information.

The two reports have to be considered as process reports. The versions of 2002 and 2003 have much of the same content and the same structure. The report from 2003 is presented as only a revision of the first report. It is not a Report to Stortinget and it is unclear what status the reports have had apart from serving as national *education at a glance* documentation, a kind of summary. The Report to Stortinget nr. 33 (About the resource situation in school and more…) (Norge. Utdannings- og forskningsdepartementet, 2003) serves as some kind of end documentation of the *School Knows Best* project. The Standing Committee asked the Ministry to report on the resource situation in the education system and a report was submitted in 2003. The *About the resource situation in the school system and more* report summed up much of the political reflection in the two reports from the *School Knows Best* project. In the introduction to the second edition in 2003, the purpose of the report was presented:

Based on national and international surveys and research as of June 2003, the present document outlines important challenges posed to the Norwegian school system. The ambition is to contribute to a knowledge-based understanding of the reality of the challenges and alternative solutions in Norwegian basic education (Norge. Utdannings- og forskningsdepartementet & Skolen vet best, 2003, p. 3).

The disposition of the reports from the *School Knows Best* project hints at a new perspective on the education system. The first chapter, *Our potential is high*, emphasizes that Norway uses more resources for education than any other country in the world. The second chapter, *Results can be improved*, presents international research on student achievements, revealing that Norwegian performance is lower than the average. The third chapter, *Money is not enough, but necessary*, presents international research that reveals the weak correlation between input and output. The fourth chapter, *How to create a good school?*, emphasizes the school as the responsible unit in the education system. This structure in the report underpins its argument, i.e. despite all the resources expended, we are still underperforming compared to other countries. We have to change the way we are governing and steering the system, from input to output. The second edition has a more aggressive critique of the national education system and uses common public perceptions and beliefs regarding the causes of the low performance of the system as arguments for change. Both reports deal with the shortcomings of the system.

6.1.1 Educational Accountability Scenarios

The *School Knows Best* reports of 2002 and 2003 did not discuss or problematize in depth scenarios for the education system. To illustrate the potential of the education system, the reports make reference to the Norwegian PISA report that described the economic and social framework that the Norwegian school system has:

- Norway is one of the richest countries in the world, if not the richest
- Few countries are using more resources on schools and education
- A unified school ideology has characterized the Norwegian school system for over 100 years – and education for all has been one of the main goals for the system
- Norway has a population of highly educated citizens and reading competence is at a high level compared to other countries (Norge. Utdannings- og forskningsdepartementet & Skolen vet best, 2002, p. 10).

The underlying argument is that in view of the national economy, Norway should have a better education system than the PISA results reveal. *Education at a glance* is presented as a status update of the education system, but the status presented to some extent reflects a particular scenario for the education system.

6.1.1.1 Knowledge-Based Economy – Nation at Risk

The reports from the *School Knows Best* project didn't convey a clear "nation at risk" message. There are no references to a risk of economic decline due to short-comings in the school system, but the presentation of the results of international student achievement tests can be understood as a kind of nation at risk presentation. The nation, despite its economic advantages, is not able to use its access to resources to develop an education system that has the same quality as nations that struggle to finance the public school system. But the underlying perception is that economic decline is not a credible scenario; a poorly performing school system is probably not able to threaten the oil-based economy. There are no discernible signs of national anxiety.

6.1.1.2 Function of Schooling in the Knowledge Society

The part played by schooling in the knowledge society isn't an issue in the reports in the same way as it is in the political groundwork documents that followed. The knowledge society is not used to legitimize the policy or set up scenarios for the education system. The function of schooling is analyzed in terms of what is understood as school quality, i.e. the main function of schooling. Developing basic skills is described as the core objective for schooling and the reports argue why:

> Often surveys of school quality are criticized for being too narrowly directed towards the basic skills of students. The reason, however, that it is first and foremost the basic skills in these subjects that are studied is the importance of these skills. For instance, students who do not read relatively fluently when they leave primary school may get problems in many subjects as teaching in higher forms is increasingly based on the use of written material. Consequently, failing reading abilities are not only a problem in themselves, they also give the students in question additional strain by making other subjects difficult for them (Norge. Utdannings- og forskningsdepartementet & Skolen vet best, 2003, p. 14).

So basic skills are held to be the main tool for all further learning:

> Implied in the criticism of using learning outcomes in basic subjects as a measure of the quality of the school system is that there appears to be a notion of a negative trade-off between basic skills and other aims like well-being, social skills, attitudes and engagement (Norge . Utdannings- og forskningsdepartementet & Skolen vet best, 2003, p. 14).

The report argues that there is no such negative trade-off. Teaching the new generation basic skills is the fundamental function of the school system.

6.1.1.3 Erosion of Trust – Shortcomings

Until 2001, Norway had only participated in three international comparative student achievement studies: in 1990–91, the International Association for the Evaluation of Educational Achievement (IEA) studies of reading among 9- and 14-year-old students, which placed Norway around the average; in 1995, the IEA TIMSS, which revealed that Norway was at the average; and the PISA in 2000, which again revealed that Norway was around the average. The *School Knows Best* reports used the international student achievement test to describe the situation in the Norwegian education system. The paradox of the unified school system is emphasized. There are strong correlations between social economic status and results, and regardless of the "all in the same school" organization of the unified school system, low-income families are not able to benefit.

Results from PISA were presented in detail to give an assessment of the Norwegian school system. The aim was to establish a "... knowledge-based reality understanding of the challenges and alternative solutions for the Norwegian school system" (Norge . Utdannings- og forskningsdepartementet & Skolen vet best, 2002). The reports focus on international student assessment studies "... and those surveys are the only information we have on outcome until a national quality assessment system is in place" (Norge . Utdannings- og forskningsdepartementet & Skolen vet best, 2002). The shortcoming that was highlighted in the report was that almost 20 percent of the students only scored at the lowest and second lowest level in reading on PISA in 2000 (Lie & Programme for International Student Assessment, 2001). At the same time as these shortcomings were presented in the report, the Minister of Education underlined *in the introduction* the success of the Norwegian school system:

> We have every reason to be proud of the Norwegian school system, but we shall not conceal that there are challenges. All the time we must work for development and improvement. It is my wish that this document may contribute to a constructive debate on how we may create an even better school in Norway (Norge. Utdannings- og forskningsdepartementet & Skolen vet best, 2003, p. 3).

This double communication is more evident in the second edition from 2003. The system is doing well, there is *every reason to be proud of the Norwegian school system*, but at the same time, there are serious shortcomings. Mistrust directed at the system is aimed at the national level and the report does not target quality differences inside the system.

Nevertheless, it has to be taken seriously that many Norwegian students do possess relatively weak basic skills. The two last big international studies of students' skills in the basic subjects – PIRLS and PISA – were carried out in 2001 and 2000. PIRLS surveys the reading abilities of 10-year-olds in 35 countries. The Norwegian results are around the international average, but behind all countries that it is reasonable to compare Norway with (Norge . Utdannings- og forskningsdepartementet & Skolen vet best, 2003, p. 5).

The report from 2003 sums up the shortcomings of the system:

In short, what we know about quality problems within the Norwegian school system:
• Far too many students do not acquire the absolutely basic skills;
• It is especially boys, minority language students and students from homes with few educational resources who are in danger of failing within the Norwegian school system (Norge . Utdannings- og forskningsdepartementet & Skolen vet best, 2003, p. 6).

Even if the reports were supposed to be empirically based, these shortcomings are explained by pointing to the Norwegian progressive pedagogic tradition. This was attacked, not only by using empirical material, but by rhetorical reference to the domestic school discourse that often is based on subjective observations and assumptions.

According to Hustad, the faulty learning outcomes are due to what he calls progressive-romantic pedagogy, where the children are seen as vulnerable and are protected against demands and the setting of limits. He criticizes the authorities for having done a disservice to the students by substituting the school of general public education with a school of upbringing and care (Norge . Utdannings- og forskningsdepartementet & Skolen vet best, 2003, p. 32).

The report also attacked common pedagogical methods in the Norwegian school system and framed this in an international critique of progressive pedagogics.

The reports A Nation at Risk from 1983 and Better Schools from 1985 were published in the USA and England respectively. The American document establishes that the educational basis of society is eroded by an increasing wave of mediocrity. The English document blamed progressive pedagogy for the insufficiency of the educational system, because it provided the students with too much freedom of choice. Progressive pedagogy was also criticized for stressing social relations at the cost of factual knowledge, and for neglecting the transfer of basic values and national culture (Norge. Utdannings- og forskningsdepartementet & Skolen vet best, 2003, p. 20).

By referring to the US and UK contexts, the progressive pedagogic tradition in Norway is offered as a possible explanation for shortcomings in the education system. Some of the references and literature used in the report are not to be considered as research, but rather as part of a political discourse. In the introduction to the report, the Education Minister Kristin Clemet emphasizes that the policy has to be knowledge and research based, but the report tends to use highly controversial sources. The unified school system is also attacked by referring to an article by Tjeldvol and Welle (2001):

> They claim that populist educational policies during the last half of the 20th century are the reason for the reduction in quality within the Norwegian school system. These policies are characterized by anti-intellectual attitudes, where practical skills and local knowledge are regarded as more important than formal knowledge and basic skills. Learning in the form of play and practical work is looked upon as more important than systematic and goal-oriented construction of knowledge among the students. Furthermore there is a strong orientation towards not creating losers, by not recognizing differences, by not using competition and by not drawing attention to the specially gifted students (Norge . Utdannings- og forskningsdepartementet & Skolen vet best, 2003, p. 33).

The paragraph can serve to illustrate a typical conservative position and understanding of the challenges in the Norwegian unified school system. It also draws on criticism of Norwegian egalitarianism, i.e. not only emphasizing that all are going to get the same opportunity, but also the same results. A focus on equality is held to hinder the development of the system and the individual student. The Norwegian school system is, according to this view, afraid of defining expectations that could create losers.

6.1.1.4 Lack of Efficiency

The report has a whole chapter entitled *Money is necessary, but not enough*. The main point made is that other countries that are considered poor are doing much better than Norway. To be average isn't good enough for Norway, when "... many poor countries such as Cyprus, Indonesia and Venezuela [...] and the neighboring countries Sweden and Finland are on the top of the ranking lists" (Norge . Utdannings- og forskningsdepartementet & Skolen vet best, 2002, p. 14).

> Material resources and social conditions cannot explain the partly weak learning outcomes within the Norwegian school system. Norway has good conditions for creating a school of quality. Norway is a rich country with highly educated adults. Few countries spend more money on school than Norway (Norge . Utdannings- og forskningsdepartementet & The Situation in Primary and Secondary Education in Norway, 2003, p. 23).

The point is that there is a weak relationship between resources spent and outcomes. Such arguments and perspectives are well-known (Eric A. Hanushek, 2003) and have been used to support the argument that there are limits for an input-based education policy.

> The Norwegian education policy debate has mostly concerned itself with the supply of more resources. We have shown that the Norwegian school system has tremendous

resources, but produces average results. The fact that there is only a small correlation between resources and results is not only a Norwegian phenomenon. A lot of research effort has been used to find a connection (Norge . Utdannings- og forskningsdepartementet & Skolen vet best, 2002, p. 15).

The rest of the chapter presents selected research that underpins the low correlation between what society is spending on the school system and outcomes. Most of the sources are British and American, but research from Norway related to class sizes and results is also presented.

> Norwegian research confirms international findings. Lately we have had the results from the research project From resources to results. The study was carried out in 1997–2002 and involved 3000 students in the 9th and 10th grades. Only one percent of the differences in results were explained by variations of resource inputs (Norge . Utdannings- og forskningsdepartementet & Skolen vet best, 2002, p. 7).

6.1.2 Educational Accountability Policy

In the introduction to the report submitted in November 2002, Kristin Clemet, Minister of Education, set out the thinking behind the new policy:

> If we are going to get better results, we have to make fundamental changes in the way we govern Norwegian schools. Previously we have emphasized too much detailed top-down regulation of the use of resources and processes. Our own experience and international research reveal that this doesn't work well enough. We have to decentralize responsibility, enhance quality control and give users more influence. The schools have to be steered bottom up within the framework of nationally defined objectives. The purpose isn't to save money, but to get more out of the resources that are already available (Norge . Utdannings- og forskningsdepartementet & Skolen vet best, 2002, p. 3).

The report looks back to the OECD report from 1988 and points out that during the nineties, a series of political documents envisaged a national system to measure quality.

> For many years there has been a political intention to develop a national system to measure quality in the school system. The work started with the OECD report from 1988 concerning the Norwegian school system. All the Reports for Stortinget nr. 33 (1991–1992), nr. 47 (1995–96) and nr. 28 (1998–99) have suggested a national system to measure quality. Despite all these intentions only fragments of such a system are in place (Norge . Utdannings- og forskningsdepartementet & Skolen vet best, 2002, p. 20).

The report argues for a shift from an input-based steering of the system to an output-based steering model. This requires that the school organization makes decisions related to the input or process and that the state transfers power to parents and local authorities.

6.1.2.1 From Input to Output

In the chapter concerning the shortcomings of the system, it is underlined that we do not have much information about quality. The assessment that was put in place in the 1990s did not assess learning outcome: final exams were evaluated on the normal distribution system; the reading test was a diagnostic test and did not focus on student learning outcome; the math tests could be presented on the national level, but did not have a design that allowed them to identify quality at school level, etc. All the effort during the 1990s to establish a quality assessment system had avoided the design that was essential for an educational accountability system, i.e. student achievement tests as a test of school quality.

> Lack of knowledge about quality is a very big problem for the local education authority and the schools in question. Ultimately it is a problem for students and parents, who do not know the level of the students' achievements, and therefore do not have the best basis for getting engaged in processes that may make the school better, or choosing another school, if possible (Norge. Utdannings- og forskningsdepartementet & Skolen vet best, 2003, p. 41).

The report emphasizes that the lack of information about output makes it difficult for local authorities as well as for parents to judge quality issues. The report underlines the international trend toward student achievement tests.

There is an international trend in educational policies regarding opening up of schools for more transparency for the authorities, the parents and the public. The core of the new national assessment systems often consists of standardized tests in central subjects, and the fact that the results from every school are made public. By making the school's results visible one wishes to mobilize for responsibility to a higher degree on all levels – both internally in the school and with the help of external pressure (Norge . Utdannings- og forskningsdepartementet & Skolen vet best, 2003, p. 42).

So the report argues that the international trend is toward transparency regarding results. Transparency will foster responsibility at all levels in the system. Output is considered to be an external pressure that might replace the input-based steering model. School is assumed to be aligned to external pressure rather than input steering by means of national learning plans. The input-based steering model is considered a hindrance for quality development at the school level.

> Furthermore, rigid rules about how education is to be organized may obstruct a good use of resources. Examples of such rules may be the size of the class, distribution of

subjects and lessons, demands about methods and the teachers' contract of employment (Norge . Utdannings- og forskningsdepartementet & Skolen vet best, 2003, p. 5).

Input policy is even considered an encumbrance to the effective use of the resources in schools and the many national regulations governing the system were criticized. And with reference to international research, the report argues for a more output-based policy.

> It is a clear finding that when the central authorities establish the curricula and are responsible for the central exams and assessments, then student achievement increases. It also does so when the rest of the decisions on the running of the school are left to the school itself. Findings from the PISA study point in the same direction, and the report refers to the fact that many of the countries that did well in the study, during recent years have changed focus from input, in the form of resources and the contents of the school, to results (Norge . Utdannings- og forskningsdepartementet & Skolen vet best, 2003, p. 37).

6.1.2.2 From Professional Community to School Organization

Even the name of the project, *School Knows Best*, emphasized the organizational level. It wasn't called Teachers Know Best. The input-based policy from the state level was supposed to be replaced by policy created by the individual school organization, and autonomy would not be autonomy for the individual teacher, but autonomy for the schools. The report pointed to the lack of authority in the school organization:

> In Norway the individual school leader has little authority to decide how to manage and organize the most important resource in school – the teachers. With a greater degree of freedom for school leaders it naturally follows that they have to take responsibility for results and can be rewarded if the results are good (Norge . Utdannings- og forskningsdepartementet & Skolen vet best, 2002, p. 39).

The report does not directly attack the power of the teachers, but the suggested output-based steering model leaves most decisions to the school level, not the teacher level. Leaders are given a more important role:

> Therefore school leaders and local education authorities have an important role to play in the development of quality and must be given space for action in order to be able to carry out this role in the best possible way. National authorities may contribute, not only by financing the training, or by setting national goals in the form of legislation and curricula, but also by developing an infrastructure which arranges for assessment, follow-up and development (Norge . Utdannings- og forskningsdepartementet & Skolen vet best, 2003, p. 47).

The distribution of power between levels and agents in the education system is discussed in the report. The main task for the national level is to control and collect data about student quality. With reference to international experiences, free school choice is presented as a way to distribute power:

> One of the arguments for a higher degree of decentralization, free school choice and decentralized decision-making is that it fosters more variation. To a certain degree experience from five different countries confirms this assumption. The variation by organizations and corporations can act as an alternative to the state (Norge. Utdannings- og forskningsdepartementet & Skolen vet best, 2002, p. 24).

6.1.3 Educational Accountability Tools

The steering tools that are suggested in the *School Knows Best* project are linked to the belief that the school is run best by itself. The main goal is to give the schools and the local authorities room for initiative. The main assumption is that schools are accountable when they are given the space for action to carry out the business themselves. The main new policy tools that are recommended are national output assessment and decentralization of decision-making. The traditional system-wide school reforms are criticized and the effects of national development projects initiated by the state are questioned.

> In Norway today, we spend relatively extensive resources on large national development projects. These are not always very well founded on a documented need. We also know little about what effect these projects have on the students' learning. The national competence development program SAMTAK was launched in early 2000 with a time frame of three years. The program has recently been evaluated. Lie et al. (2003) show that the schools to very varying degrees manage to make use of the big national development projects, and that perhaps it is time to think anew concerning school development (Norge . Utdannings- og forskningsdepartementet & Skolen vet best, 2003, p. 44).

6.1.3.1 Student Achievement Tests

Lack of information about the quality of the education system is, according to the reports, the most crucial shortcoming in the steering system. The schools did not have any knowledge about their own quality. Parents did not know the level of achievement of their children compared to children in other schools and therefore did not have a sophisticated basis to engage to improve their own school or to "… choose another school if possible" (Norge . Utdannings- og forskningsdepartementet & Skolen vet best, 2002).

We know a lot about the resources expended in the Norwegian schools, but we do not know much about the results, either in respect of learning outcome or other objectives. International studies have helped us to reveal the quality of the system, but that's not enough.

The school institution is obligated by law to evaluate itself and the school owner is supposed to see that evaluation is conducted. Only half of municipalities have systematic quality monitoring of their schools. Norway is among the few Western countries that do not have a national system for quality evaluation other than final exams.

Lack of knowledge about quality is a major obstacle for the local school owner and the single school. It is a problem for parents and students, who don't know if their school is good, and it is a problem for central government that is supposed to create education policy (Norge . Utdannings- og forskningsdepartementet & Skolen vet best, 2002, p. 23).

The report that was published in 2002 refers to the subreport submitted by the Committee of Quality (Søgnen & Kvalitetsutvalget, 2002). Based on the recommendations of the Quality Committee, the *School Knows Best* report from 2002 divided quality into three dimensions: *learning outcome, learning environment,* and *learning resources.* Structure, process, and outcome quality, which were the dimensions identified by the Committee for Quality, are here understood as learning resources, learning environment, and learning outcome.

Experience from other countries shows that publication of results in itself can stimulate effort at schools that score low. This effect can be strengthened by relating different incentives to the assessment results, also called "high-stake" testing, but it can also have some unintended consequences. The core of the system is constituted by national tests of the students' basic skills, motivation and learning strategies, and also assessment of the learning environment by students, parents and staff. There is an international trend in educational policies regarding opening of the schools for more transparency for the authorities, the parents and the public (Norge . Utdannings- og forskningsdepartementet & Skolen vet best, 2003, p. 42).

The results in themselves are believed to start a quality-developing process in the individual school. Transparency is viewed as an international trend to give central stakeholders insight into the quality of the school system.

6.1.3.2 Identifying the Failing Schools

It is interesting that the first political groundwork document already takes the view that there is not much difference in quality between schools in Norway. By making references to the Norwegian PISA report (Lie & Programme for International Student Assessment, 2001), it establishes an understanding that the

Norwegian education system is in a unique position, where quality differences between schools do not exist.

> Segregating also happens in the Norwegian school system by virtue of parents' choice of living area, and the PISA report reveals that there are few differences in results between schools. On the other hand there are considerable differences inside schools. This underlines the central value of instructional quality in the classroom (Norge . Utdannings- og forskningsdepartementet & Skolen vet best, 2002, p. 17).

Quality difference is linked to social differences between students. The PISA report is again used as the main reference to underline that despite the unified school system, social background plays a significant role.

> The averages conceal the great variations that we find among Norwegian students. Contrary to what appears to be a widespread view, the differences are greater in Norway than in most countries that we like to compare ourselves with. Research is not unequivocal as to where the differences occur: PISA shows that there is little difference between schools, but great differences within the schools (Norge . Utdannings- og forskningsdepartementet & Skolen vet best, 2003, p. 15).

The PISA report from 2001 is used to confirm that there aren't any significant differences between schools in Norway. One of the main beliefs behind educational accountability policy in undermined by the Norwegian PISA report from 2001. The *School Knows Best* report presents a national assessment system as an educational accountability system. And the report also discusses the logic of the system.

> Assessment and publication of results is not the end of the quality process, but the start. The single school and the school owner have to act based on this knowledge. Besides action that the schools themselves undertake, active parents and local politics can motivate the school for change. Central government also has the role of inspection, support and guidance (Norge . Utdannings- og forskningsdepartementet & Skolen vet best, 2002, p. 5).

A new understanding of how to steer and govern the education system is described in this short paragraph. The state level is to relinquish its role as an agent for school development, but will conduct inspections and provide support. The role of the single school, and its parents and owner, is to be responsible and to make changes based on results. It is clear that assessment isn't a goal in itself or primarily as a starting place for national reforms, but rather an incentive for development at the school level.

6.1.4 Review

The *School Knows Best* report set out to describe the current situation in the Norwegian school system. It was a politically charged document. Its structure and the issues that are discussed point in one direction: Norway needs a national educational accountability system and this requires a student testing system, results at the school level, and their publication as an incentive for improving the education system. It also describes free school choice and how parents can act as informed consumers in an education market. In an appendix, an overview of free school choice policies in other countries is described without this policy being directly recommended.

Scenarios for education in the knowledge-based economy aren't outlined at all in the report. The *School Knows Best* project was not intended to raise issues related to the function of schooling in the knowledge society or ideological questions. Core facts were set out as arguments in themselves. Absence of knowledge about quality is seen as a hindrance to developing the education system. Neither the consumers (the parents) or the government have enough knowledge about quality at the school level to make decisions. Though schools were obliged to conduct evaluations, they did not comply.

The *School Knows Best* report represents the first phase of the Norwegian movement toward a cross-national educational accountability policy. The report makes references to such a policy, but does not describe clearly the political intentions behind the system. It neither refers to "accountability" nor is anyone held responsible for the lack of results in the Norwegian school system. It is not a "gloves off" policy that is presented, but a simple logic is outlined: despite using a lot of resources in the school system, we are getting poor output and we need to assess more to ensure that we are getting what we are paying for. The second report (2003), which is more trenchant in style, argues that progressive pedagogics are failing.

The first report from the *School Knows Best* project mainly deploys economic arguments. It is more or less a cost-effect evaluation of the Norwegian education system. It targets the traditional input policy and argues that money or input isn't enough; it claims that it isn't possible to pay one's way out of failure. New policy has to be established to make schools responsible for their output.

The first report differs from later reports by introducing a form of marketization of the sector, referring to international examples of free school choice systems. Research that shows positive effects of free school choice is presented. This policy element seems to have been abandoned in subsequent political documents and processes. The educational accountability policy that is presented in the flush of the Norwegian accountability reform drive is close to the economic tradition represented by the most cited scholar in the report, Eric Hanushek. It isn't a nation at risk or unequal education opportunities that is the scenario, but the high cost and low income that are the main focus. From an economic viewpoint, the results from PISA reveal the poor effectiveness of the Norwegian education system. This is the core issue in the report. There is little mention of possible consequences other than waste of resources.

The first report almost entirely analyses Norwegian schools and school policy with reference to international research, while the second report aims to point out weaknesses at the school level using research conducted by Norwegians in the Norwegian school context. One viewpoint at the time was that Norwegian schools were focusing too much on methods and activities, leading to the neglect of learning goals. Reforms during the 1990s and the national learning plan of 1997 emphasized the project method. The national learning plan from 1997 even gave steering signals on how much time schools should give to the project method. This activity-driven planning of instruction was criticized and this was used as one of the explanations offered for the poor results from PISA in 2001.

> Researchers find that it is often unclear what is supposed to come out of the various activities in the form of learning. Some teachers have vague expectations and standards, and are reluctant to give corrective feedback. Hence the students miss out on many opportunities for learning, and it is reasonable to believe that they acquire a mistaken understanding of their own efforts (Norge . Utdannings- og forskningsdepartementet & Skolen vet best, 2003, p. 6).

The student evaluation tradition in Norwegian schools has been strongly steered by relative evaluation, i.e. what is expected of the single individual level, and evaluation has not been connected to objectives defined by a standard (E. L. Dale & Wærness, 2002). Subjective evaluation was considered to be the principal method in the education system. Common explanations are used to explain the low results: *low motivation, low expectations, low competence among teachers, lack of incentives, low self-correction at the school level*, etc. The chapter ends with a clear signal: *This may indicate that an external element should be introduced in order to obtain a positive developmental spiral in the school. Such external elements may consist of openness, external evaluation, and follow-up.* External evaluation and openness are expected to spark a positive developmental spiral in the school. The accountability dynamic is described as openness, external evaluation, and follow-ups. It is aligned with international accountability policy as the answer to the crisis in the education system.

The report from 2003 has an English version. One of the sections is headlined as accountability, but this isn't elaborated in the text. Under the heading, the international trend for more transparency is outlined; openness around results can act as a pressure to mobilize for responsibility. Openness is here defined as external pressure.

> By making the school's results visible one wishes to mobilize for responsibility to a higher degree on all levels – both internally in the school and with the help of external pressure (Norge . Utdannings- og forskningsdepartementet & The Situation in Primary and Secondary Education in Norway, 2003, p. 42).

6.2 The Committee for Quality in Primary and Secondary School Education: *First Class from First Class: A Proposal for a National Framework for Quality System*

The Committee for Quality in Primary and Secondary Education was appointed with a Royal Resolution on 5th October 2001. The Labour government resigned a week after this after losing the election in September. The new Conservative government added new members but did not change the Committee's mandate in December 2001.

In March 2002, the Committee was asked to submit a subreport and recommend a framework for a NQAS for primary and secondary education. This reflected a political shift, evident in the *School Knows Best* project, to develop and implement a national accountability system. The Committee submitted a proposal for a national quality system in the Report to Stortinget *First class from first year* in 2002 (Søgnen & Kvalitetsutvalget, 2002), and the main report *In the first rove* (Søgnen & Kvalitetsutvalget, 2003) was submitted in June 2003.

In a two-paragraph letter (March 2002) from the Ministry of Education to the Committee, an additional mandate was stated.

> The Committee should in the subreport describe, analyze and assess the current system for mapping and assessing the quality in primary and secondary education, including reporting at national, regional and local level. This has to be viewed in the light of international projects and initiatives in the field (for example projects run by the OECD) and systems for quality assessment developed in other countries.

> The Committee should propose a framework for a comprehensive approach to quality assessment for primary and lower secondary education, including reporting and follow-ups. The Committee should review the premises that have to be embedded in a national quality system that entail the national, municipal and local level, and the responsibility between the levels. The Committee should review how the national quality system should contribute to quality development on all levels.

The Committee should propose necessary action to realize a quality system. The subreport has to be submitted before June 15 2002.(Clemet, 2002)

The mandate given by the Ministry of Education linked the development of a system of quality monitoring to international education policy. The Ministry emphasized that the system had to be built on experiences in the OECD and countries that have developed a national assessment system. This is not to be misunderstood: Norwegian education policy has to connect to international trends and establish a national accountability system. The Committee had to deliver a proposal for a NQAS that entailed both reporting and follow-up. This is a clear connection between the new mandate and the positions in the *School Knows Best* reports.

The Committee had only three months to finish the subreport and the sense of urgency after the PISA shock was visible in the additional mandate given by the Ministry. After a decade of discussions on the issues, it was time to establish an educational accountability system in Norway. The Ministry used the already appointed Committee to come up with a proposal as part of their work. The report that was submitted to the Ministry on June 15th 2002 was relatively short, at 68 pages, and was divided into three main topics: *A description of the current situation, Understanding of quality in primary and secondary education, and Proposal for a national system for quality assessment and reporting/follow-up*. The current situation was summed up in six headings:

There is a lack of systematic data about the results of instruction in a form that the schools and school owners can use.

The schools and the school owners do not systematically use surveys and learning-supporting tests.

There is a lack of tools that can give the school owner a better basis for assessing the results and processes of instruction.

School owners lack follow-up in school-based evaluation.

Norway is one of the few countries in Western Europe that lack a national system for quality assessment.

A national system for quality assessment will have to make the school owner responsible as a guarantee for good schooling (Søgnen & Kvalitetsutvalget, 2002, p. 9).

The Committee came to the not surprising conclusion that the nation did not have a system for collecting data on the results of instruction in a form that schools and school owners could use in decision-making. There was no systematic use of screening or achievement tests and there were no tools available for the school owner to assess results and processes in schools. School owners were not connected to the school-based assessment that some schools conducted and did not have the insight needed to follow up the results of school-based evaluation. Again, Norway was one of the few Western European countries that did not have a national system for quality assessment. A national system for quality assessment had to make the school owner the main responsible or accountable unit in the education system. The overall picture that the committee painted was well known and the conclusions were the same as the OECD had presented in their review more than a decade before (OECD, 1989b).

> The Committee conclude that despite the last decade's decision to establish a national system for quality assessment in Norway, it is still not established. Furthermore we started a range of efforts that increasingly focus on quality and quality assessment, but follow-up on the results and quality assessment is failing (Søgnen & Kvalitetsutvalget, 2002, p. 17).

The Committee conclude that Norway has not, despite political intentions, been able to develop a national system that provides information on the quality of the system.

6.2.1 Educational Accountability Scenarios

Reflection on the function of schooling did not feature in the additional mandate concerning a national assessment system that was given to the Committee. But such reflection would be a basis for arguments about the necessity of developing and implementing a NQAS.

6.2.1.1 Knowledge-Based Economy– Nation at Risk

In the introduction to chapter two, the Committee relates the challenges in the education system to the emerging knowledge-based society. The Committee uses the knowledge-based society as a reference point for current and future challenges for mass schooling.

> The development of the knowledge and information society has contributed to the rise of competence as an important future resource and input factor that has to be managed in the best possible way. The importance of developing a high-quality education system is emphasized as crucial because education today involves all and implies a long-term perspective (Søgnen et al., 2002, p. 10).

The relation between schooling and the scenarios of the knowledge society is seen as an issue of quality in the report. It outlines political expectations that should inform schooling in a knowledge-based economy. The system has to have high quality, and competence is seen as essential capital for the future and the decisive factor for economic growth, but the nation at risk paradigm is, for all that, not evident in the subreport. Economic and global competition between states is not mentioned, but the PISA results that were published only months before are perhaps the (unstated) premise. The need to link Norwegian education policy to international policy seems to reflect anxiety about falling behind in international competition. So the additional mandate and the sense of urgency conveyed in the report reflect a perception of risk on the part of political leadership, but the shortcomings of the system are not presented as a threat to national economic prospects.

6.2.1.2 Function of Schooling in the Knowledge Society

The Quality Committee underlines that *what* has been regarded as quality in schools has depended on challenges that society faces. The underlying message is that changing challenges, related to the emergence of the knowledge society, demand new thinking about quality and thereby the function of schooling. In the chapter *What is Quality in Instruction?*, the report refers to the International Organization for Standardization (ISO) definition of quality: "Quality is the totality of characteristics of an entity that bear on its ability to satisfy stated and implied needs." According to the Committee, it is not possible to use the ISO definition because needs related to instruction and schools will always be contested. Three perspectives on quality assessment are offered in the report: (1) the legal (whether schools satisfy the regulations that they are steered by), (2) schools' response to expectations from society, and (3) quality criteria based on professional judgments. The Committee does not take any position on different approaches to quality issues, but in their conclusions, it is the expectations from the society that are emphasized as the measure of quality.

> In Norway, as in other countries, the understanding of what is regarded as quality in the education system has changed over time. It has depended on what problems society and the educational sector have identified at any given time (Søgnen & Kvalitetsutvalget, 2002, p. 6).

When the Committee suggests that the main problem with the Norwegian school system is the lack of focus on basic skills, this reflects what is seen as society's requirement, a focus on basic skills. The function of schooling that is implied is to secure the development of basic skills.

6.2.1.3 Erosion of Trust – Shortcomings

The issue of a lack of trust is not problematized in the report. The emphasis on better steering and transparency may reflect concern about trust, but the Committee seems to avoid the issues related to the erosion of trust. The issue seems implicit too in the discussion of challenges schooling will encounter in the knowledge-based society. The Committee points out that the Norwegian education system has traditionally disregarded quality related to output and student achievement. They do not attribute blame, preferring to argue that until now the system has emphasized structural issues and process quality, so that there has been little effort devoted to issues of output quality. The Committee points out that Norway has not had a system to monitor output quality: "Norway is one of the few countries in Western Europe that do not have a national system for quality assessment of primary school" (Søgnen et al., 2002). But a lack of trust in schools and teachers is evident in the Committee's thinking about a new steering system. The Committee redefines the role of the school owner. In the Norwegian school system, the municipality as a school owner has had a limited role. School results should be used as steering information, and the school owner is assigned a new role in the subreport. This is a matter of sanction; the school owner as the responsible unit in the new system has the responsibility of acting if schools do not meet quality standards. The professional community's role as the guarantor of quality is not seen as reliable. Schools are to be responsible and the school owner has to act if expectations are not met. In this sense, the erosion of trust is implied, but not clearly articulated.

System-wide school reform is not seen as a route to better quality. All the agencies that have had central roles in the system are now set aside. It is the organization of the school and municipal government, which have had a more or less invisible role in the development of the educational system, that is now given the task of turning the system around. Reliance on the state level as a school owner, developer, and reformer is clearly put into question when the Committee proposes a narrowing of the Regional State Education Office's mandate in respect of monitoring.

6.2.1.4 Lack of Efficiency

The lack of effectiveness in the education system, which was the main focus in the *School Knows Best* reports, is not an issue for the Committee. Correlation between resource outlays and results, or the lack of such a correlation, is not discussed in the report. There are no references made to education economics or inefficacy issues.

6.2.2 Educational Accountability Policy

The new policy that the Committee discusses has a clear enough logical stance: we do not have information about the quality of the education system when quality is understood as students' basic skills. We need this information to be able to steer and govern the system. The new policy is centered around a national assessment system and the intention is "that a national system for quality assessment will put quality on the political agenda in each individual municipality and region – and for the public and local politicians" (Søgnen & Kvalitetsutvalget, 2002, p. 16). The public will be mobilized and will be engaged in issues of school quality. School quality, understood as output quality, will be part of local policy discourse.

One of the odd twists in the report from the Quality Committee is that it is not the school that will be the accountable unit. It is the school owner or local authorities that will be made accountable. "A national system for quality assessment has to make the school owner responsible for good schools" (Søgnen & Kvalitetsutvalget, 2002, p. 14). It is an educational accountability policy that is indicated with the difference that school owners will be accountable. In traditional educational policy, the owner or the public sets up systems to make schools accountable. In Norway, the state is to set up an educational accountability system that will make the local democratic system accountable for school results. It is not the schools themselves that are responsible for output, but the local community represented by local democratic institutions. Accountability is located in the authority that provides the input (school authorities at the local level) and not the individual schools that are supposed to provide output quality.

All the same, the report presents a policy that embodies core tenets of international educational accountability policy: a shift from input to output, emphasizing school organization and decentralization.

6.2.2.1 From Input to Output

The Committee adopts the main assumptions in the *School Knows Best* reports, i.e. that Norway has a strong tradition of input-dominated education policy. This tradition has had no focus on system output. The state has had information about how municipalities or school owners provide resources for the schools, but very little knowledge about the results obtained:

> In general, the overall picture is that we collect detailed information on input factors and have little information about the relation between instruction and learning and the results of instruction. This has made it difficult to provide the necessary information to plan and work strategically with the quality of instruction (Søgnen & Kvalitetsutvalget, 2002, p. 14).

Information is needed to plan and work strategically to enhance the quality of instruction. The address for such information is quite unclear. When the responsible unit is the school owner the main address for planning and strategic effort is probably the school owner.

> Nations have planned education on a huge scale from the beginning of the 19th century. It was first in the 60s that planning for education in most countries set out to secure all children a basic education, first in primary and lower secondary school. The focus has primarily been to channel expenditure in relation to school building, access and teachers. In practice this has resulted in a detailed overview of the volume of students, teachers, building facilities, and the ratio between the different inputs (Søgnen & Kvalitetsutvalget, 2002, p. 14).

The main assumption is that as long as the local political level does not have any insight into school quality, then school quality will be a real political issue. The lack of interest in school output quality is due to the absence of relevant information. When the local authorities can have access to relevant information, provided by the state, then school quality can emerge as a political question at the local level. The Committee does not envisage a local demand for, or interest in, school quality.

6.2.2.2 From Professional Community to School Organization

There is no discussion of the school as an organization. The Committee does not communicate any trust in the school organization as an agent for change. There is no notion of a transfer of power from the professional community to the school organization.

6.2.2.3 Distribution of Power

The Committee emphasized that a new system for quality assessment would have to have the local democratic level, the municipalities, as its starting point. School owners lack information about quality in their schools. Information about the quality would give them tools to steer their schools. It is the political level in the municipalities that should be responsible for acting on the basis of the new information.

6.2.3 Educational Accountability Tools

The tools that the Committee recommend for Parliament are aligned with international accountability policy: achievement tests, publication of results, and follow-up based on these results. On the other hand, the dynamics that would emerge in the wake of the policy are treated as unintended consequences. The Committee presents two arguments for a national system of quality assessment, one related to improvement and the other related to accountability.

Another argument for quality assessment that is relatively seldom used in Norway is the idea of a kind of obligation for accounting to society, so-called accountability. Internationally accountability is used in many contexts. The concept is used in pure financial terms as "value for money" or in a political context it is related to the idea of the authorities' democratic right to control systems that are to serve society. A school system is viewed as accountable, efficient and of high quality if it meets the needs and demands of its users (Søgnen & Kvalitetsutvalget, 2002, p. 5).

The Committee offers both arguments and explanations. The explanations offered seem ambiguous, almost as if they do not support the policy, but all the same offer a rationale:

In addition to these arguments, the increasing need for assessment of quality can be explained by:

- A renewal of the public sector that emphasizes quality and access
- Compulsory schooling as a foundation for work and further studies
- Meeting the demand for a skilled workforce
- Producing information and facilitating information for users and the public
- Information for different steering levels – state, municipal and school
- As a basis for discussion about improved efficiency
- Norwegian school in the context of international society
- As a basis for further reform (Søgnen & Kvalitetsutvalget, 2002, p. 24)

So the Committee does argue for a national assessment system, but offers some explanation of such a policy. The tools that are suggested are not outlined and grounded in beliefs held by the Committee. It is as if they only see the need for assessment of quality as a product of external forces affecting the system, and not as a precondition for system change and improvement. But the explanations offered are in reality all strongly linked to the belief that the school system will have a central and increasing strategic impact in society.

6.2.3.1 Student Achievement Tests

The Committee points out that Norwegian education policy has traditionally focused on structure and process quality rather than student learning output, i.e. quality has been linked to how instruction has been conducted rather than to outcomes.

The national student achievement tests are the main tool that the Committee suggests to the Parliament. The Committee distinguishes between three kinds of quality in education, pertaining to structure, process, and outcome. Structural quality is the total framework for schools: financing, steering documents, competence, buildings and equipment in place, etc. Process quality is understood as the quality of relations and processes inside schools. It points to matters of content, method, and the opportunities provided for professional development. The learning environment is a central factor in process quality. Result or outcome quality is what the students actually have learned, the competence they have acquired during their time in school. The Committee affirms several times that student achievement or product quality is the main indicator of school quality.

> With result quality as the principal benchmark in the assessment system it is student output that is going to be assessed, and will point toward what is regarded as quality. There are many possible ways to measure output quality (Søgnen & Kvalitetsutvalget, 2002, p. 27).

Outcome or result quality is to be the main criterion for assessing what is considered as quality in the education system. The Committee looks at different possible ways to assess outcome quality. Social competence and learning strategies are examples of outcomes that should be included in the assessment system. They are central objectives in the national learning plan and should be considered important outcomes. The Committee discusses different achievement or quality tests: national tests, sample tests, and exams. They propose national tests and argue that this type of test, for all students, gives a more precise picture of students' learning outcomes and can monitor development for the whole country. In addition, it is possible to compare the results of local, regional, national, and international tests over time. National tests are resource demanding and the secondary school has a tradition of national exams that can overload the system, according to the report. It is possible that the national tests can replace the grading and exam system. The Committee argues against the grading and exam system and does not consider it adequate for measuring and comparing learning outcomes related to basic subjects or basic skills. They refer to international research that implies that the Norwegian school system has to enhance the quality of basic skills in Norwegian schools. The basic skills are considered to be the foundation for learning in all subjects. An alternative approach is to conduct national tests in basic skills or key competences such as reading, writing, and skills in second languages at different levels in primary and secondary schools.

The Committee is quite specific in its proposals for the organization and in its conduct of national tests in basic skills. National tests should aim to test students' learning outcomes in knowledge and skills, but the system should start with assessment of basic skills in reading, writing, math, and English communication skills. The main goal, to have a holistic assessment, i.e. knowledge, skills, and beliefs, is not mentioned in the proposal for the concrete achievement test system. The extent of testing is narrowed down to the second and fourth year in primary school, the last year in lower secondary school, and the second year in higher secondary school. The tests are national in the sense that they are going to be comprehensive for all students in the specific school year. The tests in second year primary school should focus on reading and the tests in the fourth year should focus on math. The committee emphasizes that testing has to make it possible to see the connections between national assessment and the international student assessment tests that Norway participates in. That means that international tests can at some time replace national tests.

The Committee concludes that student achievement tests or learning outcome tests are the most precise tool for measuring quality in the education system, but structure and process quality has to be added. Structure and process quality is more or less considered to be an added value factor, as additional information for analyzing outcome quality. Structural quality can be viewed as an input factor and process quality targets the organizational level in the planning and conduct of instruction. Both dimensions mirror the school-based evaluation tradition that has had firm roots in Norway. Traditional pedagogical values in Norway have emphasized schools as a resource in the local community, collaboration between teachers, how students are involved in the planning of instruction, and collaboration between schools and the local commerce.

The accountability system that is proposed in the subreport does not deploy any sanctions. The Committee underlines that the new system conveys a pressure on all levels in the education system to improve quality. The Committee emphasizes that the results should be available for the public. The system has to meet demands and expectations for information and transparency that are characteristic of contemporary society. And it is a challenge to define sanctions, first because quality is hard to define, and secondly because a national system for sanctions will impact upon local autonomy.

There is dissent in this part of the report. A member of the Socialist Party Rolf Jørn Karlsen, Ragnhild Lied from the teacher union, and the Labour Party politician Anikken Huitfelt did not follow the majority. They disagreed about the proposal of a national assessment system that would only entail the control dimension, and wanted a system that would embrace both control and development. The focus, according to them, should be on development. The division of responsibility between the national level and the local/school owner level was in this sense disputed. The dissenters argued that evaluation had to be understood as either market oriented or professionally oriented. A market understanding of evaluation and assessment would be focused on the control dimension and professional assessment would emphasize development. The dissenters wanted to avoid the political steering of the school system being located in an assessment office, beyond political control. They objected to changes that would result in steering signals about learning in schools increasingly being provided by a quality assessment bureau rather than being informed by objectives defined in the learning plan.

One chapter of the subreport is devoted to describing the Quality Web Portal. Its purpose would be to provide the school owner and the individual school with information as a basis for local quality assessment and quality development. It should be possible to compare the information that is provided by the student achievement tests. A generic principle for the web portal is transparency: the portal should be open to the public, but ranking lists should be avoided. The single school should be able to compare its results on structure, process, and learning outcome quality on five levels: with other schools in the municipality, with other schools in the country, with an average for the schools in the municipality, with an average for comparable municipal groups, and with the national average.

The Committee emphasizes that the portal should be accessible for the public, but that the information should not be presented in ranking terms. The portal should, in the view of the Committee, not create A and B schools, but focus on the development of schools. All the quality indicators related to structure, process, and outcome are supposed to not be suited to a lay ranking and grouping of schools.

6.2.3.2 Identifying the Failing Schools

The PISA report from 2001 is again the main reference for the assumption that there are no failing schools in Norway; it is maintained that there are no quality differences between schools, or that the differences are more significant inside schools. The correlation between SES and results is understood as a problem inside schools and in the classroom. Differences in quality between classrooms are not problematized or used as legitimation for the new quality system. The publication of the results does not set out to identify failing schools.

> The results from the study show that Norwegian students achieve above average compared to the OECD average. The Committee has noted that:
> – There is no great difference between schools in Norway, but there are surprisingly great differences between classes in the same school.

The Committee believes that the PISA study points to tendencies that are important to take note of. The Committee wants to emphasize the considerable differences in student achievement between school classes inside schools (Søgnen & Kvalitetsutvalget, 2002, p. 29).

There are no arguments or explanations offered for a national assessment system linked to quality differences between schools and unequal education opportunities due to these differences.

6.2.3.3 Decentralization

The Committee distinguishes between evaluation/assessment and guidance. The school owner, i.e. the municipality, is responsible, according to the Education Act, for evaluating the individual schools. The state level is responsible for the assessment and guidance of schools through the Regional Office for Education, which represents the state at the regional level. The Committee underlines that there is not a complete mandate for school assessment and that there are considerable variations in practice between the Regional Education Offices, municipalities, and schools. The Committee argues that evaluation and guidance should be improved by a national system for quality assessment. The national system has to be built on some generic principles: school owners as the main responsible institution for quality at the school level and the state level as the facilitator for the national system for quality assessment. The national level has to provide information about the quality of the education system and the school owner is asked to analyze and follow up the results. The regional level does not have any responsibility in the new structure and the Committee proposes that the offices should be reorganized and absorbed into the state regional administration (*Fylkesmannen*). The Regional Education Offices will be confined to conducting inspections related to national regulations.

The Committee presents three target groups for information from the assessment system: the state level, school owners, and the single school. Quality assessment as defined by the subreport has to contribute to information addressed to two main groups: users and participators on the one hand, and decision-makers on the other hand. The Committee identifies common needs: the need to monitor developments, to identify improvement areas and what could enhance quality, to determine what areas should have the highest priority, and to determine to what degree instruction can contribute to motivation and well-being.

In addition to the different stakeholders who need information, different levels are also identified: the school level, the school owner level, and the state level. Quality assessment, according to the Committee, has to reflect the different interests in, and demands for, assessment, depending on the level in the education system.

At the school level, the Committee distinguishes between different stakeholders: students, parents, teachers, and school leaders. At the school owner level, there are two main groups: the municipalities and the regional political level, the owners of the higher secondary schools in Norway. At the state level, the assessment system must inform user groups that manage and steer the education system at the national level. The Committee outlines the different needs in respect of information for stakeholders on the three levels.

The school leaders, students, parents, and teachers are regarded as being at the same level, the *school level*. Students need information about their own development in the learning process so that they can make decisions, prioritize, and have a real influence on their own learning process. Parents need information about the range of aims and objectives that are embedded in the national learning plan. And parents need information about the content and the organization of the instruction given in schools, and the students' learning output and development in the framework of a broad understanding of competence, i.e. knowledge, skills, beliefs, and values. It is interesting to note that the Committee does not assign parents any role as decision-makers based on the information. The parents need information to be able to understand, not to decide. On the school level, teachers need to collect and share information about the planning, conduct, and evaluation of instruction. The information that this process requires, according to the Committee, is the quality of the learning environment, learning process, and output, so that the teachers are able to inform and guide the students, parents, and school leaders. The school leaders need steering information about the learning environment, the organization of instruction, progress in the learning process, and output at the group level and the single student level to make the right decisions about the use of resources and to conduct leadership. In addition, according to the Committee, the school leader needs to be informed about the situation at the school level so that they can prioritize adequately.

The school owner level has to have information to ensure that students are getting the instruction they are entitled to regarding the national learning plan. That includes offering the resources and competences that are necessary for instruction, but also for evaluating and developing the schools. School owners, according to the Committee, need information about the total situation at the single school level to put into action the necessary measures. The Committee added school leaders as a key factor for all three quality dimensions. The quality of the school leadership is seen as crucial for student outcomes.

6.2.4 Review

First Class from First Class appears to construct a new form of external educational accountability system that embraces more features and involves a broader quality concept than traditional accountability systems set out to do. By including process and structure quality, the system seems to account for factors other than student achievement tests when testing schools. When the proposal is boiled down to what is going to be put into action, it is an ordinary and more or less traditional accountability system that emerges, i.e. students will be tested in basic skills at the end of school years 4, 7, and 10, the results will be published and made available for the public, and there is an assumption that being at the low end of the scale will motivate the schools to improve.

The proposal also adds a bureaucratic structure that is necessary to create the dynamic of the educational accountability system. The political level in the single municipality is put in the front seat as the school owner. The municipality is not only hosting the schools, it is also going to actively evaluate the schools and follow up the results.

The scenarios of education outlined in the proposal are aligned with the new accountability system. The school system is not criticized for lack of quality, but rather the need for schools to relate to society's expectations, society being understood as the knowledge society. The main objective for the school system is to secure the development of the capacity to learn, i.e. developing competence in basic skills. Basic skills are defined as the centerpiece of the system.

The achievement test system that is suggested is supposed to serve all levels and the Committee has the ambition to create achievement tests with multiple functions. Some functions may be impossible to incorporate in one single system. A clear understanding of the function and purpose of the evaluation system is, however, lacking. The First Class from First Class report is quite short at 60 pages.

By only presenting arguments and explanatory material for an educational accountability system, the Committee was not forced to take any positions related to function and purpose. Some of the explanations presented do reflect on the function of schooling and are highly controversial within the Norwegian school policy tradition; for example, seeing the school system as a provider of the workforce can be viewed as a reduction of the function of schooling to only respond to demands as defined by what is most economically efficient. The Committee does not legitimate the proposal of an accountability system by pointing to the explanations they offer. They relate to matters more or less beyond the control of the school system and the system only will have to adapt, but the Committee doesn't take any position on these issues.

Accountability/responsibility and the need for *quality improvements* are the two evident arguments that the Committee is using to legitimate the implementation of an external assessment system. Accountability is linked in the report to steering and the demand for transparency in the democratic system and does not reveal any positions taken on the function of schooling other than what can be related to expectations or the demands from society. The assessment system could result in improvements in quality through creating a *desire in schools* to enhance student achievement and to reveal areas that need improvement. It will contribute to assessing teacher competence, and implementation, and encourage the use of new methods and variations in learning methods. It underlines that an assessment system in itself does not contribute to quality improvement, but the system has to entail guidance, professional development, monitoring, and sometimes a case for increasing the resources available. The two arguments are of course connected: the desire to improve quality based on information about the quality of student outcomes and external pressures are by no means discrete entities.

The quality argument, on the other hand, is related to instruction and the level of proficiency in basic cultural skills, i.e. the report does not bring into question the overall quality of the school system. It is the lack of *basic cultural skills*, such as reading, math, writing, second languages, etc., that is in focus, as well as the consequences for society and the individual when the development of such skills does not meet expectations.

The system that is recommended sets out to ensure that schools work toward the essential object of securing proficiency in basic skills among the Norwegian student body. The Committee underlines that basic skills are an individual as well as a societal aim. There is no conflict since the aim serves both the individual and the collective level.

A performance-based accountability system has to select what to test. The process of selecting the content or skills that are tested reflects the position taken on the function of schooling. By ranking and defining the desirable output, the function of schooling is revealed. The competences that the Committee wants to test are cross-subject skills. The purpose of schooling is to secure basic skills and the school subjects or content are ranked as a part of the method rather than carrying an aim in themselves. That means that basic skills are not viewed as a single subject aim, but are placed above all the objectives that are linked to the single subjects. Lifting the *basic competences or skills* out of the single school subject and setting them forth as an objective for all subjects embodies a transformation to the core function of schooling defined as a provider of basic skills as tools for all further learning. The other subjects are regarded as material to learn rather than objectives in and of themselves. Learning to learn then becomes the legitimation and platform for integration and inclusion for compulsory schooling. It is not the catechisms or the history of the national state that are to be tested. Mass schooling as a tool for securing certain beliefs and values is no longer the yardstick for quality. The quality of schooling is the degree to which the school is able to develop basic skills. The quality concept in the report narrows expectations for schooling down to cognitive abilities that will be required in the future.

In the knowledge economy paradigm, the quality concept that the Committee espouses is inclusion by virtue of the ability to learn. In the history of the development of mass schooling, teaching of basic skills has been one of the main functions of schooling, not seen as a route to inclusion in itself, but as an entry to the religious or national community. Inclusion in the development of mass education is linked to the existence of educational objectives or content that are regarded as so valuable that everyone, irrespective of background or future role in society, had to acquire them. The institution of compulsory schooling in Norway was motivated by the perception that the lack of basic reading skills among the public that were needed to conduct religion in the Protestant ethos was disabling, i.e. the personal relation between the individual and God. Confirmation was the rite of passage and the qualification for becoming a full member of society. Inclusion in society in the ethos of the knowledge economy is being able to participate in a lifelong learning process, i.e. learning to learn.

A performance-based accountability system is not the source of the transformation of schooling, but a sign of that transformation. The function of schooling in the knowledge economy society is narrowed down to learning to learn and requires that these skills be tested.

In addition to the two main arguments for the new quality system, quality improvement and accountability, the Committee adds six explanations or rationales that support the need for quality assessment: renewal of the public sector; schooling as a requirement for further education and work; meeting the need for a competent workforce; collecting and organizing information for users (parents and students) and the general public; the need for information for steering and decision-making at all levels – the state, municipality, and the single institution; and initiating processes to make the system more cost-effective, to make the Norwegian school system viable in international society, and as a necessary basis for new school reform.

6.3 The Committee for Quality in Primary and Secondary School: *In the First Row*

The Committee for Quality in primary and secondary education submitted its main report in June 2003. Parliament discussed the report in the following autumn. While the subreport from 2002 only consisted of 40 pages that aimed to outline a national quality system, the main report had over 300 pages, and discussed in depth some of the issues that were only dealt with superficially in the subreport submitted the year before.

The report contained proposals covering most issues in the education system: structure, teacher education, finance, etc. The mandate for the Committee was broad and the Committee had to interpret their mandate. They defined five focus areas:

The main report will develop perspectives in the subreport, in particular:

- Emphasizing learning output and the coherent competence that the instruction should target.
- A focus on basic skills.
- Emphasizing the role of the teacher as the key factor in instruction.
- Underlining the school owner's role as a guarantor of quality in schools.
- The value of evaluation and documentation as a foundation for quality and development (Søgnen & Kvalitetsutvalget, 2003, p. 33).

The original mandate that was defined only days before the Labour Party left office in 2001 was no longer of any importance. Moreover, the main report had emphasized the additional mandate submitted in 2002 by the new Conservative government. The extent to which the Committee managed to emphasize these focus areas is, however, questionable.

6.3.1 Educational Accountability Scenarios

The main report from the Quality Committee discusses the scenario for education in greater depth. Scenarios describe the challenges ahead and act as a legitimation of the policy that is proposed. It is not a nation at risk that is described in the report. The education system is described as being in good health and international studies such as PISA are scarcely mentioned in the report. The main task for the education system in the knowledge-based paradigm is presented as learning to learn and the fundamental tools are the basic skills. The relatively large amount of resources expended in the system and the questionable quality of the system in itself is not an issue in the report, but there are no arguments for more resources.

6.3.1.1 Knowledge-Based Economy – Nation at Risk

The report links the quality of the education system in a nation and the nation's ability to compete in the global economy. Competence is defined as the capacity to use knowledge to cultivate human capital. The knowledge economy paradigm is described, but there are no signs of a nation at risk perspective.

> In addition to being buildings, educational institutions are to an increasing degree a fundament for economic growth. Globalization of the world economy and the decline of the traditional industrial labour market has put competence policy at the top of the political agenda in many countries. In the competence economy it is the capacity to use knowledge, i.e. systems to distribute knowledge to relevant receivers and cultivate human capital, that is the important factor that determines our capacity to compete in a global economy (Søgnen & Kvalitetsutvalget, 2003, p. 33).

So the drive and motivation for focus on the quality of the education system is linked to the emerging knowledge society and globalization.

> Norway is part of a larger world society. The knowledge society is global. Globalization will put the quality of the educational system at the center, also in Norway. We compete with other countries in the education market, and this means that our own education system will have to have high quality to compete (Søgnen & Kvalitetsutvalget, 2003, p. 44).

The Committee does not convey any direct criticism of the current education system aligned with the new paradigm, but it does emphasize the need for quality. Education, and the quality of education, is crucial in the ethos of globalization and the knowledge society.

> We do have our own unique education culture that has many positive features, but it is also important to admit that it is always possible to do things even better, and that we can learn from other countries (Søgnen & Kvalitetsutvalget, 2003, p. 44).

But even though education and schooling are placed at the center of development in the knowledge-based society, the responsibilities that devolve in the system are not articulated. There is no sense of urgency.

6.3.1.2 Function of Schooling in the Knowledge Society

The function of mass schooling is an important issue in the report. The learning to learn paradigm is connected to most issues that are discussed. Learning to learn is described as being proficient in basic skills.

> The changes in society in the last 10–20 years have seen the emergence of a "knowledge society" and the information society is being transformed into a competence society. This development has led to an increase in understanding of the notion that

fundamental values in society do not primarily derive from book knowledge, but rather through capacity and motivation to acquire new information, knowledge and skills by virtue of own lifestyle and personal initiative. The broader application of the concept of competence has to be seen as a logical and natural consequence of this development (Søgnen & Kvalitetsutvalget, 2002, p. 11).

Mass schooling in the knowledge society is presented as part of a never-ending learning practice in all parts of society and the report describes a change of aim for mass schooling, that is, to integrate new generations in learning practices rather than to integrate them in a given body of knowledge. The focus on basic skills as the fundament for all further learning and integration is evident in the report. Mass schooling is to be restricted to the acquisition and development of basic skills. The report uses the concept "basic competence" to describe the goals for mass schooling and defines this basic competence as *basic skills, social competence, and the development of learning strategies*. But it does not set out to describe this new ground for schooling in any detail.

> The committee wants to emphasize that the education system, to a much greater extent, will have to focus on students' basic competence and that this basic competence will be basic skills, social competence and development of learning strategies. Digital competence is to be put on a par with skills in writing, reading and maths. The Committee proposes that this basic competence should be integrated in the entire learning plan for subjects. This is a central point in the report (Søgnen & Kvalitetsutvalget, 2002, p. 12).

Basic competence is elevated to be the main issue in all subjects. A learning plan above all other learning plans is established and the goals are related to the ability to learn. This isn't an extension of the existing content in mass schooling, but rather a narrowing of the main expectation for mass schooling in the knowledge society, i.e. learning to learn. It is not a back to basics approach, rather, it is a new approach that is adjusted to the new scenarios for the knowledge society.

6.3.1.3 Erosion of Trust – Shortcomings

The report describes the Norwegian school system as a success, but with some shortcomings related to learning of basic skills and the lack of monitoring of learning outcomes. These shortcomings, when they are mentioned, are often linked to international trends. Failures are not due to the exceptional education tradition and policy in Norway, but are to be found in most education systems and are related to the development of the knowledge society.

6.3.1.4 Lack of Efficiency

The money is not enough perspective does not play any role in the report. Quality or lack of quality isn't discussed in relation to the amount of resources that are spent in the Norwegian education system. There are no discussions of the inefficacy of the system.

6.3.2 Educational Accountability Policy

Education policy in the report regarding educational accountability policy is strongly related to the quality assessment system that was under development.

6.3.2.1 From Input to Output

When the Committee interpreted their mandate, there was a clear shift of focus from input to output. All the issues that the Committee defined as the core for their mandate were related to a more output-oriented policy. Even the main input, the quality of teachers, was related to output.

- Emphasizing learning output and the coherent competence that the instruction is targeting.
- Focus on basic skills.
- Emphasizing the role of the teacher as the key factor in instruction.
- Underlining the school owner's role as a guarantor of quality in schools.
- The value of evaluation and documentation as a foundation for quality and development (Søgnen & Kvalitetsutvalget, 2003, p. 33).

From input to output is often described in the report as a natural law that impacts on the school system. In view of the goal-oriented steering paradigm in the public sector, the implication is that the education system has to adjust to this policy. The issue is not dealt with in terms of the need to give the schools responsibility for creating a practice that can enhance output quality. As a consequence of the new paradigm, new tools for measuring output have to be developed. "A prerequisite for goal-based steering is the development of measuring and follow-up tools" (Søgnen & Kvalitetsutvalget, 2003, p. 250). There are no arguments in the report that underpin the need for more output-oriented steering.

6.3.2.2 From Professional Community to School Organization

The school as an organization is hardly mentioned in the report. The organization is not described as a tool for school development. It is the single teacher and the school owner, the municipality, that are regarded as the main responsible units in the system. The school as an organization is an issue in the chapter dealing with the role of the teacher. In the short subchapter *Toward a learning organization*, the school organization is not understood as a tool for quality development, but more as a setting in which teachers can reflect on the role of education in society.

> Reflection in this context can be understood as self-reflection, a self-renewing doubt of proficiency in understanding and solutions. This entails knowledge and practice having to be continually critically analyzed to assess if they are adequate for situations and challenges in the future (Søgnen & Kvalitetsutvalget, 2003, p. 63).

The school owner has to ensure that the single school is becoming a learning organization.

> The school is responsible for the students, who are the reason for the existence of the organization, that they should obtain, develop and create a series of competences over the years. How the school is working is crucial for how the single student is to experience the years of instruction as meaningful and successful (Søgnen & Kvalitetsutvalget, 2003, p. 245).

6.3.2.3 Distribution of Power

The Committee does not describe a new form of power distribution. Parents are mentioned, but as a resource for the school and not as agents of choice. How the new educational accountability system is going to challenge the traditional power distribution is not discussed in the report. A new form of power distribution related to parents and students is not evident in the text.

There is no suggestion that parents and students should have an opportunity to choose between schools. The results of students' achievement tests are not going to give parents a right to move to a better school.

6.3.3 Educational Accountability Tools

The educational accountability tools that are described in the report are mostly a repetition of the description given in the subreport. The function of the system is treated in depth and new functions are added.

6.3.3.1 Student Achievement Tests

The Committee elaborates the description of the student achievement test system. The structure and content of the system are described as proposed in the subreport, but the Committee adds and enlarges upon the purpose of the tests and it seems as if the function of the test system has evolved in a somewhat different direction. How the test system is going to be able to cover all the functions that are described, by both the Committee and the Ministry of Education, is not seen as a problem. The issue is not discussed in the report.

Tests
Tests are seen as diagnostic tests. "The Committee suggested in the subreport the establishment of national tests in central subjects. The tests are to replace both diagnostic and national surveys" (Søgnen & Kvalitetsutvalget, 2003, p. 227). The question of how a national test system could act as both a diagnostic and a national survey is not dealt with. The different designs that might be required related to the function of the tests are not mentioned.

Data-drivendecision-making
In the same chapter, the Committee refers to how the Ministry of Education defines the function of the tests related to the written budget proposal to Parliament:

> The Ministry suggests that the tests will serve different purposes. They will give decision-makers at different levels in the education sector a foundation for necessary action, and give students and parents a better basis to participate in improvements in instruction (Søgnen & Kvalitetsutvalget, 2003, p. 227).

There is a belief that the same tests will give parents a more significant role in the development of the school.

As a final exam
The Committee suggests, with two dissensions, replacing the final exam in the 10ᵗʰ grade with the national tests and other local assessment tools.

> Considering the structure of the education system, the committee does not see the need to keep the final exam in the central subjects Norwegian, Maths and English. ...The Committee thinks that national tests have embedded functions that more or less replace the final exam (Søgnen & Kvalitetsutvalget, 2003, p. 230).

The national test will also serve as an individual exam at the end of lower secondary school. In addition, the results will be a mark that decides entrance to the higher secondary school system.

Not only skills
Tests are not only going to test the basic skills, but also students' insight and ability in using knowledge and skills in other contexts.

> The results from the test will serve to assess developments over time related to students, teachers, school leaders, school owners and the national level. The tests are not only

going to test students' knowledge and skills in a narrow way, but are going to reveal understanding, insight and the ability to use knowledge and skills in new contexts (Søgnen & Kvalitetsutvalget, 2003, p. 227).

These claims about what assessments the new tests will support are ambitious. It is as though the Committee is arguing on the basis of criticism directed at the first report and adding new functions to the assessment system. How the tests could be designed to be able to reveal all this information about output at different levels is not an issue in the report.

Feedback to students

> Two paragraphs later: "the tests are going to serve two functions: as a tool for assessment of schools and to give the students feedback on their level and learning output" (Søgnen & Kvalitetsutvalget, 2003, p. 227).

This confusion about the function of the student achievement test system colors the entire report. All known purposes related to testing of students are assigned to the new national test system. The Committee emphasizes that the tests have two main functions: to assess the school and to provide feedback for students. If the school is the central influence on student output, feedback to the students has to be related to the influence of the school upon their attainment.

6.3.3.2 Identifying the Failing Schools

Again, the PISA report from 2001 is used as proof that there aren't any quality differences between schools in Norway. It is interesting how the Committee explains quality differences as being related to Socio-economic status, and thereby as a factor beyond schools' control. The strong correlation between results and SES are not attributed to low school effect.

6.3.3.3 Decentralization

Decentralization is described in relation to the change from input steering to output steering of the education system.

> The demand for goal- and result-orientated steering at the executive level entails more responsibility for schools. Decentralized steering demands higher competence further down in the organization. A focus on output and learning requires goal-oriented development and competence at local level. Both leaders and teachers need to increase their knowledge about how satisfactory results are to be obtained by means of innovation. This is an important challenge for a decentralized school system that has changed its focus from input to output (Søgnen & Kvalitetsutvalget, 2003, p. 246).

So the Committee asserts that schools need more competence when the steering system is more decentralized. It is interesting that the school is not treated as an organization, but as an enterprise consisting of teachers and leaders. Both, according to the Committee, need more knowledge about how to attain their goals.

6.4 The Report to Stortinget: *Culture for Learning* – 2004

The Report to Stortinget no. 30 (2003–2004) *Culture for Learning* (Norge. Utdannings- og forskningsdepartementet, 2004) provided a summary of the school policy that had been developed by the Conservative government after 2001. The starting point was the *School Knows Best* project in 2001, leading through to the Quality Committee in 2002–2003 and in 2004 to the report *Culture for Learning*.

The Minister of Education Kristin Clemet presented the White Paper *Culture for Learning* as her education policy manifest.[3] The report stated three preconditions for the development of the education system: *Knowledge*, related to a NQAS; *Competence*, related to teacher training, training of school administrators and leaders, competence development, and advice and support from local and national authorities; and lastly, *Culture for learning*, related to local freedom of action.

6.4.1 Educational Accountability Scenarios

The report points to the role of the education system aligned with new demands from the knowledge-based society. At the same time, it is not a nation at risk of economic decline that is described.

6.4.1.1 Knowledge-Based Economy – Nation at Risk

The knowledge-based economy is used in the report to underpin the need for change, but it isn't a Nation at Risk paradigm that is presented in the report. Norway is presented as doing well and there is no reason to believe that this is not going to continue.

The knowledge-based economy is outlined when the report concludes that the ... *most important input factor in working life is competence*. This underlines the role of education in the knowledge-based economy.

---

3   Dagbladet 26 August 2004.

6.4.1.2 Function of Schooling in the Knowledge Society

The function of schooling in the knowledge society is aligned with international trends. The report suggests adjusting our expectations of the school system and focusing or narrowing down the main function of schooling to the development of basic skills as a foundation for lifelong learning. *Culture for Learning* conveys a clear understanding of the function of schooling in the knowledge society. The concept of basic *skills* is replaced by the basic *competences* that were proposed by the Quality Committee. Basic skills are defined as tools for learning and development. They are cross-subject objectives and all subjects in school should aim to secure the basic skills defined as "to be able to express oneself orally, to be able to read, to be able to express oneself in writing, to be able to do arithmetic, to be able to use information and communication technology" (Norge . Utdannings- og forskningsdepartementet, 2004).

Learning in the knowledge society is also a goal for other institutions as well as schools. Therefore, schooling is only a preparation for further learning in the knowledge society.

> Learning proceeds in many arenas, and it is important to create a foundation for lifelong learning. This means that we must change our expectations directed at the faculty in terms of instruction and have more rigorous expectations for the school as an arena for developing basic skills (Norge . Utdannings- og forskningsdepartementet, 2004, p. 9).

The new function of schooling in the knowledge society also demands, according to the report, a new model for steering the system.

> To make schools able to meet the challenges from a more knowledge-driven society, a system change is needed, where steering is based on clear national objectives, a clear location of responsibility and increased local freedom of action. Through the national system for quality assessment, the school will acquire knowledge that can be used as a starting point for change and development. To use this knowledge in a constructive way, the schools need competent teachers and school leaders that have positive beliefs in respect of development and change (Norge . Utdannings- og forskningsdepartementet, 2004, p. 5).

Narrowing of school content and objectives is aligned with international trends that see schooling as an integral part of a learning society.

6.4.1.3 Erosion of Trust – Shortcomings

The shortcomings that are described are related to poor achievement in basic skills among Norwegian students. "Research reveals that many students do not develop necessary basic skills during their education" (Norge. Utdannings- og forskningsdepartementet, 2004, p. 9). The focus on these shortcomings is aligned with the new function of the education system in the knowledge society paradigm. There is a clear assumption that many students underachieve and complete their schooling with poor results.

Culture for Learning does not offer a consistent explanation for the situation in the Norwegian school system as evidenced by poor performances in international student achievement studies. It describes a failing school system rather than failing schools. In the short chapter *Possible Causes For Lack of Learning Outcome*, four main explanations are offered: unclear objectives, a high degree of teacher autonomy in determining content, an absence of focus on learning outcomes, and low expectations and weak leadership. All these are well-known features in poorly performing schools. The chapter does not seem to acknowledge that some schools most certainly are doing well and some schools are performing poorly. One of the core assumptions behind an educational accountability system, quality differences between schools, is lacking.

> In contrast to common opinion the proportion of weak students is higher than in many countries we would want to compare ourselves with and also higher than in countries where social inequality is greater than in Norway (Norge . Utdannings- og forsknings-departementet, 2004, p. 14).

Despite the fact that students perform poorly compared to other countries, the school system is presented as well-functioning. The shortcomings are not attributed to inefficiency or a lack of proficient teachers; it is instead a lack of focus and steering that is the problem. There are no references to earlier school reforms that failed to target the problems. The school system has only failed to adjust to the new demands from the knowledge society. In addition, the school system has, up to the present, been steered by the state in a manner that does not meet the needs of a knowledge society. Schools have to start focusing on learning outcome. This isn't an attack on progressive pedagogics or a criticism of teachers or schools. The system is doing well and can do better. There is no note of urgency in the report.

6.4.1.4 Lack of Efficiency

The money is not enough argument is not articulated in the report. It is as if the money is not enough argument has been attacked and the point that very considerable resources are deployed in schools, which was a mantra in the *School Knows Best* report, is absent. The Ministry seems to argue against some common explanations of the high-cost system.

> Among OECD countries there are few states that spend more money on education in terms of expenditure per student. Norway also has the highest ratio of teachers per student and this is the main reason for the high costs. Both in the biggest cities, the towns and in rural areas there are many teachers in relation to students (Norge . Utdannings- og forskningsdepartementet, 2004, p. 16).

The economic perspective presented in the *School Knows Best* report is not used as an argument for reforming the system when the policy is summed up in *Culture for Learning*. Nor are there any references to a lack of incitement for the system to perform.

6.4.2 Educational Accountability Policy

The education policy presented in the report is aligned to cross-national accountability policy. Politicians are going to define the objectives and measure the learning outcome. When the schools are going to be accountable for their students' learning outcome, it is necessary that most decisions are made inside schools. The state can't dictate how schools should be run, and at the same time, make schools themselves responsible for the results.

6.4.2.1 From Input to Output

The new steering system must, according to the report, be based on five principles: clear national objectives, knowledge about results, clear division of responsibility, extensive local freedom, and a strong support and guidance system.

> The idea that the State can create an equal education system for everyone through detailed regulation and steering will be replaced by trust that the single teacher, school leader and school owner have the capacity to see how learning can be facilitated and conducted within the framework of national objectives (Norge . Utdannings- og forskningsdepartementet, 2004, p. 9).

Input policy is replaced by output policy. It is argued that deregulation is an assertion of trust toward teachers, school leaders, and school owners. They have the best capability to translate national objectives into learning outcome. That the state is going to define the goals for the activity in schools is not problematized. In the report, national regulation of school instruction is to be replaced by local freedom and the state will expect that the schools and local authorities will find better solutions that are adjusted to local demand.

> Today's detailed steering of method and organization of instruction is to be reduced and it is suggested that national norms for instruction time and subject distribution will be adjusted so that schools have more room to decide according to local and individual demands (Norge. Utdannings- og forskningsdepartementet, 2004, p. 25).

6.4.2.2 From Professional Community to School Organization

The school organization is given an important role in the new steering system. The last report from the Quality Committee emphasized that local authorities would be the most accountable unit. In *Culture for Learning*, the school is seen as the accountable unit in the system. One of the preconditions for high quality in education was culture for learning in the school organization – not only regarding the learning of the students, but also how the school organization was learning.

> The development of a more knowledge-driven society is challenging for schools in many ways. Firstly, there will be a greater demand for schools to act as learning organizations. This means that schools have to focus on the learning of their staff, and not only on the learning of the students. It means that competence has to be developed, shared and adjusted to the needs of the organization. It means again that we need to loosen up the traditional structures and methods in the schools (Norge . Utdannings- og forsknings-departementet, 2004, p. 9).

Compared to the other reports, *Culture for Learning* conveys a clear understanding of the role of the school organization in the new steering model. The school owner or the local authorities are responsible for output, but the school organization is, in the last analysis, responsible for reaching the national objectives. The school owner has its role in supporting the school more than being itself the accountable unit.

> Everyone in the organization has to take responsibility and feel obligated to realize common goals. The ability to continually reflect on whether the objectives that are defined and the choices made are right for the organization is fundamental. That is the core competence for learning organizations and is at the same time the necessary skill for the school as an organization (Norge . Utdannings- og forskningsdepartementet, 2004, p. 26).

The school organization is going to define common objectives and it is a collective responsibility to realize these. The individual professional is replaced by a school organization with a hierarchical structure. In the end, it is the school leader who defines the common interest and approach. The report makes many references to international research to support the implementation of learning organizations.

6.4.3 Educational Accountability Tools

The policy tools presented in the report emphasize the deregulation of the education system and the autonomy of the school. The NQAS that was going to be implemented is described as the core instrument in the shift in the steering policy.

6.4.3.1 Student Achievement Tests

The NQAS is not given much space in the report. The system is only mentioned three times in the report which is over 100 pages in length. A year before the report was submitted, parliament had already budgeted and negotiated the system. The decision was, in reality, already made.

> The national system for quality assessment will give information about learning outcome, resources, learning environment and well-being. It will be a tool for the individual school and school owner to gather knowledge as a foundation for development. The web portal skoleporten.no will provide transparency and facilitate the school itself, the school owner, parents, students and other interested parties engaging in the development of the school (Norge . Utdannings- og forskningsdepartementet, 2004, p. 26).

The address for the result is the public and the point is to get central stakeholders engaged in the development of the school. The school itself is accountable, but at the same time, the public and the school owner have the responsibility of engaging in the development of the school. If the school is performing very well, it is probably not necessary to engage. At the same time, the report refers to the system as the core tool in the shift of steering policy. "The national system for quality evaluation and development is part of a bigger system changeover" (Norge . Utdannings- og forskningsdepartementet, 2004, p. 9). The system was outlined in the reports from the Quality Committee and the focus in *Culture for Learning* seems to be the framework for the quality assessment system, i.e. deregulation and the school run as a learning organization.

Some of the lack of clarity about purpose or lack of knowledge about the national test system does seem to surface in the report. It is suggested that the test can replace the final exam. In the Norwegian tradition, the final exam is a test of a range of skills and knowledge. To think that a national test in basic skills could replace the final exam betrays a weak understanding of the tool that was to be implemented.

> When the national tests are implemented the amount of testing will increase, but this will also make it possible to have fewer local tests. The Ministry will continue the oral final exam, but will consider whether the written end exam can be gradually replaced by national tests (Norge . Utdannings- og forskningsdepartementet, 2004, p. 9).

The design of a student achievement test that can measure school quality would differ significantly from a written final exam. Devising a standardized test that could include the functions of a final exam would seem to be unrealistic.

6.4.3.2 Identifying the Failing School Organizations

There are no references to failing schools as a challenge for the system. The system seems to be set up to identify national challenges for which the state has the responsibility to act.

> In cases where national challenges are evident it can be necessary to adopt national strategies for special areas. These can be competence development in central areas or national initiatives to support larger development projects (Norge . Utdannings- og forskningsdepartementet, 2004, p. 26).

There does not seem to be any awareness of the pool of low-performing schools that the system will serve to uncover. Identifying failing schools as a political tool for developing the education system is not an issue the document deals with.

7. Implementing the Accountability Policy 2004–2006

After three years of political groundwork, the *National Test System*, as the main tool in the accountability reform, was launched in the spring of 2004. The test system encountered massive protest among teachers and students. What were regarded as minor nuances in the political development phase rose to the surface when the system was put into action. The centerpiece of the achievement-based accountability system, publication of the results and the possibility of comparing schools, was hotly disputed.

The implementation of the policy required that Parliament had to grant (finance) the development and implementation of the system din 2004–2006. Every time the system was granted by the Parliament, a political discussion emerged around the purpose and function of the national quality system. It seemed as if the political legitimation process, the development process, and the implementation process were going on simultaneously.

The evaluation of the tests (Lie et al., 2004; Turmo, Lie, Ibsen, & Hopfenbeck, 2005) that was conducted in 2004 and 2005 is more or less a description of total chaos: the evaluation revealed a lack of competence related to test theory and a lack of coherence in the development of the tests.

A survey of issues related to the implementation of the system among teachers and school leaders was carried out (TNS-Gallup, 2004). In retrospect, the test that was launched in 2004 and 2005, apart from some parts of the reading tests, did not have the quality or form required for a student achievement test in an educational accountability framework.

National tests were described as the centerpiece in all the political documents from 2001. The Quality Committee and the *School Knows Best* report outlined the national tests as part of a new control and steering reform, but the tests that were launched in 2004 and 2005 were more or less constructed in a form that conveyed a rejection of educational accountability and the system seems to have failed before it had even started. There are few written sources concerning the development of the tests, and the present study has had to rely on the evaluation (Lie et al., 2004; Turmo et al., 2005) and the few written sources from the different development groups.

7.1 Developing and Implementing National Tests

The Learning Centre, and the New Norwegian Directorate for Education and Training from 2004, was in charge of the development of the test system. The assignment was formulated by the subproject K for Quality as part of the modernization project *School Knows Best*. The political groundwork document didn't refer to the body of knowledge concerning achievement test-based accountability systems (Norge . Utdannings- og forskningsdepartementet & Skolen vet best, 2002, 2003; K. f. l. Norge . Utdannings- og forskningsdepartementet, 2004; Søgnen & Kvalitetsutvalget, 2002, 2003; Ødelien & Jacobsen, 2003). It didn't seem as if the Directorate had much grasp of the challenges in creating tests to measure school effect. In the framework from the Directorate of Education provided for the groups that were to devise the tests, their purpose was described in four paragraphs: to give the decision-makers at all levels information about the condition in the education system and thereby give a basis for necessary action for the sector; to give information to the users of the system about the quality of instruction in the single school as a basis for choices and making improvements; to give information to school owners, school leaders and teachers as a basis for improvement and development in the single school; to give information to the parents as a basis for learning and development and to monitor development over time, both at system and individual level.

The framework for the development of the tests can be misunderstood. In a non-externally accountable educational culture, like the Norwegian one, the framework was more or less assumed to be normal student testing in a diagnostic tradition with diagnoses reliant on explicit theory with the expectation of some prescribed solution. The tests were not set up to give some notion about what might be done at the school or school organization levels, but what to do on an individual level – the student level. The purpose of the tests described in the framework given to the development groups was *not* part of a control and steering reform. Necessary action for the sector as one of the purposes described in the framework could be understood or interpreted by the development groups as a requirement for new pedagogical or methodical approaches. A well-known position in the didactic research community is that teachers' methods in the classroom are often failing to comply with theory developed in the research community. Necessary action may be understood as action that complies with research findings. The research groups that were assigned to develop the tests represented the didactical research community – not being part of an educational testing research community, that didn't exist in Norway. Their assignment was understood as an authorization to implement new didactical theory and method, far from the original purpose of testing school quality and far from being able to produce test results that could reveal quality differences between schools. The lack of massive support for the reform might have encouraged the research groups to put aside the main political objectives, i.e. steering and control.

The research group that was to create the writing test had developed a complicated competence wheel involving seven different ways to understand and assess writing. The test had such low quality or high degree of complexity that it was not possible to publish the results (Lie et al., 2004; Turmo et al., 2005). Two of the main researchers in the group announced in 2005 that there were two ways to conduct national tests: one where all the students were tested and one where a representative group was tested (Måsvær, 2005). They admitted that it was a political decision to conduct national tests for all students, but that this wasn't necessary and it was an option that only a representative group should be measured. The subtext was that the group formed to develop the tests had understood the tests as an assessment of the national level in writing among 4th, 7th, and 10th grade students and not as assessment of schools and learning results at the school level. And it was a political decision, not their decision, to conduct a redundant test for all students; only a representative group needed to be tested. These viewpoints from members of the development groups revealed that educational accountability was rejected and the purpose of the national tests was more or less understood as an ordinary didactic research assignment.

In retrospect, the development of the tests was more or less out of control. It is clear that the Directorate failed to convey the function of the tests as they were formulated in the political groundwork documents. Even if there was political disagreement around the publication of the tests, this would not excuse a misunderstanding of the main function of the tests, i.e. output quality monitoring of basic skills.

The assessment and evaluation of the tests that was conducted by Lie showed that most of the tests could not be used as accountability tools. The research group assigned to develop the math tests had, after piloting the tests, removed all the items that were teacher dependent. This exemplifies the lack of understanding of a national testing system that has the function of identifying a lack of school effect, i.e. items that are learning dependent are desirable.

7.2 The Transformation

During the negotiation of the political groundwork documents in the parliament, the function of the national testing system was at the forefront of the discussions. The many functions of the national tests are not consistent and there is a form of transformation. In the end, even the Conservative Party doubted the value of the publication of the results. It is not easy to follow the transformation process, but from 2001 until 2004, the function of the tests was changed, going from making schools accountable to giving schools information about their own students – from testing the schools to testing the students.

During the negotiations in Parliament, there was a broad political consensus that the publication of the results was <u>not</u> going to create a ranking list of schools. How it would be possible to publish the results without being able to compare and make ranking lists was an issue that was not dealt with. It seemed as if Parliament did not see that it was possible to have transparency of the results without this revealing failure.

7.3 The Boycott

During the autumn and spring of 2004/2005, different student organizations started a campaign to boycott the national tests for the 10th grade. Some areas and school districts had such a low level of participation that the value of the system seemed to be endangered. How it was possible to mobilize a wide boycott hasn't been studied or analyzed, but the connection between final marks in lower secondary school and national tests that the Ministry of Education proposed for the 10th grade students seems to have accelerated the boycott. Student and teacher strategies for negotiation around final marks were disrupted by the state level through the national test system. Adding the final marks in the 10th grade to national tests communicated that the state level interrupted the local negotiation between teachers and students regarding marks.

The Ministry added this to prevent a boycott, i.e. you may not get final marks and the teachers could get a test for free as a foundation to mark the students, but it had the opposite result. The massive boycott was probably not a sign of political awareness among the Norwegian 10th grade students, but a response to being measured up to national standards rather than traditional single school/teacher standards. The boycott started as an initiative from a group of students in Bergen school districts, but the boycott campaign gained momentum when the test results in the 10th grade were threatening the end marks. There was already dissension regarding the publication of the results from the tests in the first White Paper by the Quality Committee. It is clear that the consensus was not real.

8. Reforming the Reform 2005–2009

> We were the first to implement national tests.
> It didn't work. We tried to make them perfect
> and took too many considerations; the effect
> was a poor result. (Clemet, 2008)

Because of the poor quality and the massive boycotts of the national tests in 2004 and 2005, it is reasonable to conclude that the attempt to implement a national educational accountability system built on student achievement tests had failed. The minister responsible, Kristin Clemet, has stated that the implementation of the national tests under her leadership was so poor that the Conservative parties felt that they did not have any authority to protest when the new government reformed the test system.[4] They had tried to construct tests that were designed to cover all intentions and purposes serving all different interests and the foundation for the national test system as an accountability tool was eroded. The accountability perspective vanished during the political processes and the political system had relied on it being possible to create tests that were able to satisfy all kinds of purposes even though that was not possible.

It became obvious that the development groups that were assigned to create the tests didn't have the capacity that was required to develop achievement tests that were able to measure school quality (Lie et al., 2004; Turmo et al., 2005). The massive resistance against educational accountability, communicated as resistance against national tests, more or less forced the Conservative coalition to make adjustments. Even if it seems like there was broad political support for the accountability reform, it was clear that the system was not comprehended by the political system as a tool to make anyone accountable, but as a tool to inform teachers and parents about their own children.

8.1 The New Coalition 2005: Soria Moria Declaration

Two of the three parties in the new red-green coalition, Senterpartiet and the Socialist Left Party SV, had made a national congress decision that supported ending the national test system and replacing the system with representative tests. When the red-green coalition won the election in 2005, Øystein Djupedal was appointed as the Minister of Education and he represented the *Socialist Party*

---

4   Kristin Clemet in Verdens Gang 23 August 2008.

in the coalition – a party that only a year before had announced in their *School Political Manifest*[5] that they were strongly against the national test system.

National test policy was an issue during the negotiation of the political foundation for the new coalition. In the declaration of the founding of the coalition, it was announced that the national test system was going to be stopped and reformed. A new political position was revealed in the *Soria Moria* declaration from 2005 that formed the foundation of the red-green coalition from 2005 to 2009.

> The government will further develop and improve the national system for quality assessment in a way that it emerges as a more accurate tool for schools, students and parents. As the aim is to adjust the instruction to the single student it is necessary that students, teachers and parents have the necessary knowledge about the students' challenges (Regjeringserklæringen, 2005).

School owners and the public are not understood as an address for the results. The purpose, as outlined in the declaration, is to disclose understanding around the single student learning challenges, so the single teachers are able to adjust the instruction to the individual student. Information around quality in the education system, which had been an issue in Norway from the OECD review in 1989, is, in a rare twist, turned to being a lack of information on the teacher level, i.e. the new coalition stated that teachers do not have or lack information about their own students' challenges concerning the development of basic skills. The national level is intervening in the classroom by establishing a mandatory national test system that has the objective of informing teachers about their own students' level in basic skills.

The teacher unions suggested in 2003 that the national test should <u>not</u> be implemented. Aligned with two of the parties in the coalition, Senterpartiet and the Socialist Party, the union recommended a representative test system, which gave a statistical basis to monitor quality on a national level; the union was against the national testing system at the school level. This position didn't surface in the Quality Committee despite the fact that central representatives from the union were represented. The positioning is also aligned with the proposal in the *School Policy Manifest* to the Socialist Party from 2004.

At the same time that the political declaration from 2005 cancelled the educational accountability reform, the declaration underlined that the national test system was going to be continued and even improved.

---

5   Skolepolitisk manifest (SV 2004).

It is going to be proposed that the current system of national quality assessment is changed in dialogue with school owners, teachers and the organizations, after an overall evaluation. The government will improve the national tests, but limit the costs and extent. The aim is to secure a more precise feedback to the schools, parents and students to test if the basic skills are aligned with the expectation that is defined in the national learning plan.

National tests will not be conducted in 2006. The test results are going to be available for the public, but they aren't going to be used for ranking of schools (Regjeringserklæringen, 2005).

By deciding that the results are not going to be comparable, the main tool for measuring the quality of the education system vanishes in the declaration. The interesting part is that the national test system was going to be continued by the new government, but the proposed construction of the system was aiming to take away the generic basis for the existence of the system. It was not the aim to measure students' achievement *against* other students' achievement, or schools compared to other schools, but to measure quality *against* the goals that were defined by the national learning plan. The learning plan was established as the standard, not other schools or high-performing schools. It is a clear intention for the new government to construct the system in a way that all accountability elements and dynamics are erupted, but at the same time, to continue the national tests.

8.2 Reforming the National Test System

The national tests were, as announced in the Soria Moria declaration, stopped in the autumn of 2005 by the new red-green coalition. Arguments behind the break were bound to the massive protests among teachers, the boycott from students, and the low quality of the tests. It was also a clear shift in policy. While the previous Conservative coalition was selling the system by under communicating the accountability dimension, the new government aimed to remove the accountability dimension. The ambition that was outlined during the groundwork was more or less abolished. Already in the declaration, a clear shift in the function of the system had been announced and the extent of the system was narrow.

In autumn 2006, new national tests were introduced and conducted, but the amount of tests and the time when the tests were going to be conducted were changed. The tests were now moved to the autumn, i.e. at the beginning of a new school level/year. While the original tests measured the end results or learning outcome at the end of the 4th grade (lower primary), 7th grade (middle school), and 10th grade (lower secondary), the tests were moved to the start of the 5th grade and 8th grade, the starting point for middle school and lower secondary school. The shift seems like a small adjustment, but the new government changed the tests by moving the time of measuring and changed them into a diagnostic tool to screen the levels of incoming students in autumn. The main purpose was to screen the students so that the teachers could adjust their instruction to the right level. The national test was defined as a common tradition of screening students starting at a new school with a new teacher. The tests were understood as a tool for the teachers to screen what was in front of them for the year – a practice and tradition as old as school itself. Teachers didn't boycott the new tests, but the tests became a part of the regular screening of new students. There wasn't any political or public discussion around the changes of the tests. When the new government changed the tests, the old one, the opposition, remained totally silent.

8.3 The Function of National Tests

Publication of the results was understood by the new government as a blaming and shaming of students. In an educational accountability system that is based on student achievement tests, the lowest performing schools will combine low instructional quality with serving low-income families. On the national level with a system without any value-added component regarding the SES of the students, the lowest-ranked schools will be serving low-income families. The logic of the system is to identify schools that don't have the capacity to bring children from disadvantaged families to a proficient level in basic skills.

The ranking system was understood by the new government as a system for blaming poor kids for their poor performance. The opposite position was the international mantra: don't blame poor kids for poor performance (Lessinger, 1970; Thrupp, 1998).

The laws that regulate transparency in public administration made it difficult for the red-green coalition to deny insight into the results. Ranking lists were published by the Norwegian media, but the lists didn't have any political tool for steering schools.

Part IV. Discussion and Conclusion

9. The Output: Similarities and Differences

Norwegian education in the period 2001–2004 saw an effort to adopt an international education policy. The documents from that period have been explored and analyzed in the context of international educational accountability policy. Similarities and differences between international educational accountability policy and the Norwegian output formulated in the political groundwork documents have been outlined and analyzed. The study has set out to show whether the core ideas and beliefs behind the policy were articulated in the documents, and whether a feasible framework for dealing with issues of school quality was put in place.

The move toward accountability structures in Norwegian education has led to controversy and some considerable confusion. One can question whether opposition to student testing and ranking of schools according to set criteria has always been based on consistent political or professional positions. Probably not, in view of the evident fact that there have been few strong, clearly profiled advocates for testing and ranking. If testing and ranking have seemed to many to be an unwarranted, overly radical departure, it is also clear that the intellectual case for accountability structures and accountability tools has scarcely impacted upon debates about school. It often seems that accountability issues are assigned to discussion within a compact professional and academic circle, while practical political initiatives have been blunted by disagreement and uncertainty, not least at the state level. As we have seen, the accountability policy's emphasis on the school and its performance, and its significance as the decisive arena where educational outcomes are determined, has not been articulated in state policy. This, just as much as a groundswell of skepticism or downright opposition to testing and ranking, has led to the adoption of forms of testing that are not fit for purpose in terms of accountability.

We have seen that the policy being developed underwent a transformation, from a recognizable educational accountability policy presented and outlined in the first reports from the *School Knows Best* project in 2002 and 2003, to what can only be characterized as a compromise in the last White Paper, *Culture for Learning*, in 2004. The two White Papers from the Quality Committee (Søgnen & Kvalitetsutvalget, 2002, 2003) were an attempt to define educational accountability in terms of the Norwegian quality tradition. The Committee rejected accountability as an option for the Norwegian school system, and instead what can be regarded as a *quasi-accountability* system was proposed, i.e. it involved all the known elements of an accountability system, but the link between these elements was not set out, and the accountability dynamic was under communicated. The Committee did not define the core function of the centerpiece of the system, i.e. the national tests. They responded to political pressure for accountability and transparency, but seemed to reject the accountability dynamic, i.e. that someone has to fail and someone has to be held to account. The fact that quality at the school level produces different results in student achievement tests was not seen as an issue. Discussions around the main assumptions or principles behind an accountability system, quality differences between schools, were not dealt with.

An external student test system was the apparent centerpiece of the new policy, with the aim of informing the system so as to make different levels accountable. Norway seemed to adopt international educational accountability policy, but at the same time, rejected the main hypotheses that the policy is grounded on. Fundamental assumptions were neglected in the groundwork documents. The result was a quasi-accountability policy with the same tools and structure as international accountability policy, but with an uncertain content and purpose (Nusche & OECD, 2011).

9.1 Education Scenarios in the Groundwork Documents

The scenario for the education system that was outlined in the groundwork documents reflected to some extent international trends in education policy in the knowledge society. But the Norwegian PISA shock did not spark any anxiety about national failure or a nation at risk. An OECD report from 2004 summed up the reaction to the PISA results in Norway:

> It is clear from the data that Norwegian pupils at age 15 underachieve in comparison with Finland and Sweden and – in certain respects – the OECD countries as a whole. Often Norway also shows a wider spread of outcomes than Finland and Sweden, similar to those in other OECD countries. Overall, these results must be seen as disappointing, given that Norway is an advanced, rich country with a strong commitment to equality and a high level of educational expenditure (Mortimore, 2004, p. 31).

The PISA results were a disappointment for Norway, but the results did not lead to any great concern, and certainly not to anxiety about the prospects for the nation to the same degree as in Germany and Austria. The results were not presented as a sign of the end of Norway's position in the global market (Lie & Programme for International Student Assessment, 2001). The "first-class view" of the Norwegian school system was challenged by the PISA results and some claims about poor instructional quality were confirmed. One might take the view that the unified school system was discredited, in particular in relation to poor results among students from low-income families. The social group that was supposed to benefit most from the unified system appeared to benefit least in the *all in one* school system (Lie & Programme for International Student Assessment, 2001). But this entirely reasonable conclusion, supported by PISA results, was not drawn in the political groundwork documents.

9.1.1 The New Paradigm – Nation at Risk

The knowledge society is a paradigm that frames a new understanding of the significant role of the education system related to economic growth and social inclusion in society in the future. Even if the knowledge-based economy was an evident scenario in all the reports, economic decline for Norway was not an issue in the documents. There was no sense of urgency as reflected in the *Nation at Risk* discourse in the US (Forente stater . National Commission on Excellence in Education & USA Research (Firm), 1984). The knowledge society paradigm in the documents was aligned with international policy, but Norway has for two generations enjoyed a well-founded oil economy that ensures economic growth – Norway does not seem to be a nation that is likely to be confronted with economic decline.

So the Norwegian discourse differs from international discourse by not focusing on the risk of economic decline if the education system isn't reformed, but is similar in its description of the significant role of the education system in the new economic paradigm. The paradigm of the knowledge economy is adopted, as in other Western countries (Mehta, 2013b), and this challenges many assumptions in traditional education policy. Even though the school is assigned a more significant role in the development of the economy, there has not been any anxiety about economic decline due to shortcomings of the education system.

9.1.2 Function of Schooling in the Knowledge Society

The definition of what was regarded as school quality in the groundwork documents was the ability and efficiency in the instruction of basic cultural skills. The basic skill *turn* reflects a shift in the function of mass schooling in the knowledge society related to learning to learn rather than representing a conservative back to basics understanding of the function of schooling (Isaksen, 2002, 2008; Luhmann, 1997; Luhmann & Schorr, 1979; Tenorth, 1994, 2004). Learning to learn or basic skills as the main objective for the school system was accepted and adopted by all political parties during the education reforms in the nineties (Aasen & Telhaug, 1999). This political consensus, related to basic skills as tools for learning, has to be considered fundamental for the development of educational accountability policy. The basic skill turn makes it possible to define a common ground on what is considered to be school quality.

The White Paper *Toward better Goals...* that was submitted in 1999 concluded that it isn't possible to define school quality; it is just too complicated of an issue (Roald, 2010). The groundwork documents and processes after the PISA shock were, however, able to define the function of schooling related to the knowledge society paradigm, i.e. the competence to learn for all.

The objectives for mass schooling in the knowledge society are narrowed down to learning to learn. Learning to learn is the central expectation for the educational system in the framework of the knowledge-based society paradigm. Norwegian exceptionalism, which had supported the view that values and goals for the national education system were impossible to measure as a basis for assessment, was actually abandoned in the political groundwork documents. Norway instead followed international trends in focusing upon and describing basic skills as the main tool for developing and acquiring competence for learning and learning to learn, this being the main function of mass schooling. This turn is essential to enacting the new policies because it makes it possible to define objectives that can be conceptualized and worthwhile to measure and monitor. It isn't basic skills in themselves that are understood as the quality or the function of mass schooling, but proficiency in basic skills is an indicator of the ability to take part, and be included, in knowledge-based societies with their continually expanding need for new orientation and innovation through learning.

Basic skills are not only understood as a starting point for instruction, but are presented as a goal for instruction in all school subjects and in all grades. What to some extent differs from international policy in the Norwegian case is that basic skills are no longer understood as basic – a starting point – but rather are skills that need to be continually trained and developed. Basic skills are seen more as a continuum for learning to learn, rather than as a starting point that is going to be attained and then left at a certain level of proficiency. Everyone is defined as an object for instruction in basic skills irrespective of their level of proficiency. Subjects are regarded more as a material for training and developing the skill to learn. All the same developments in Norwegian pedagogy reflected the emerging international political consensus regarding the main objectives for mass schooling (Luhmann, 1997; Luhmann & Schorr, 1979; Mehta, 2013a; OECD, 1996, 2001b; Tenorth, 1994, 2004), and this consensus makes it possible to agree on a quality of schooling that is measurable. By defining five basic skills as the objective across all school subjects, the proposal from the Quality

Committee and the Report to Stortinget *Culture for Learning* was aligned with international trends toward a narrowing down of school content and objectives.

Limiting the function of schooling to learning to learn in the knowledge-based society has to be considered a shift that can make it possible to legitimate a basic skill-based student achievement test as a fundament for the educational accountability system. This foundation was established in the Norwegian groundwork documents.

All the policy documents convey an understanding of the school as the central arena in a knowledge society. The increasingly political focus on the quality of the education system is presented as a result of the new role of mass schooling. In this sense, the Norwegian discourse was similar to that of cross-national education policy. Norway is confronted with the same challenges as world society and the function of mass schooling is linked to new imperatives. Schooling is a starting point for lifelong learning, rather than a place to socialize and discipline a new workforce. Failure in providing a foundation for further learning is assumed to have consequences for the development of society as a whole. Quality in school is significant for society in a new and more important way that requires us to exert more control and to monitor the quality of the education system.

9.1.3 Mistrust and Shortcomings

The Norwegian school system is presented as a success in all the central groundwork documents. The critical attitude that was conveyed in the reports from the *School Knows Best* project was dampened down after 2002. The public or official position that was established during the groundwork phase was that *we are good and we can be even better*. Questions regarding differences in quality and unequal opportunities are absent in the policy documents. The new policy isn't conveyed as a response to criticism or a failure of the policy, but as a natural development of the education system, i.e. until now, Norway has, like other countries, emphasized access for all and now we have reached this goal and are able to concentrate on quality. The Quality Committee states that the priority of input-based education policy has been correct, but now when we have attained access for all, presented and understood as equal educational opportunity, it is possible to focus on improving the quality of the system related to learning outcome. According to the Committee, it will be feasible to pursue a more output-based steering policy.

All the political groundwork documents reflected on the relation between the quantity of resources used in the Norwegian school system and the poor results in international student achievement tests. Despite all the money put into the system, the results were poor. This brought the traditional input-based policy into question; the habitual political device, i.e. transferring more resources to the system, had apparently failed. However, the *School Knows Best* reports communicated mistrust in the steering system rather than in the instructional system. A belief that the *School Knows Best* can be interpreted as mistrust in steering or of the state level and a belief in the alternative of transferring responsibility to the single school. The political will to create a system for monitoring and control reflects mistrust directed at the system.

It is very significant that the notion of *failing schools* is not articulated in the political groundwork documents. In this central issue, the documents are unconnected to the international discourse relating to failing schools and the social injustice that failing schools represent when they serve underprivileged groups. Failing schools or failing school districts are essential to the Western discourse related to mass schooling, but this has never been the case in Norway. In the history of the development of educational accountability policy, unequal educational opportunities related to differences in quality between schools are a central issue. How failing schools jeopardize social inclusion appears to be a wholly absent issue in the groundwork. The political commitment to an educational accountability system is embedded in the assumption that school quality determines educational and occupational opportunities at the individual level. When some schools are able to bring their students to a certain level and other schools with the same resources cannot, public pressure emerges to narrow the achievement gap between schools. When education quality, or lack of quality, is not linked to how schools are run and the fact that some schools are underachieving, the political and public mandate for implementing a national accountability system is missing. The naïve assumption that Norway has not had quality differences between schools has undermined the core foundation for a national student test system.

The Committee for Quality focused on basic skills as an Achilles heel for an *after all* well- functioning Norwegian education system. They restricted their mistrust to the lack of focus on instruction of basic skills. Poor performance in schools was not attributed to the lack of competence or effort in the system, but to a lack of focus on basic skills. This contrasts with international educational accountability policy in which one of the main political perceptions supporting more control and external pressure is an assumed lack of expectations and quality of instruction in schools that serve low-income families.

The political groundwork documents do not represent any shift in the focus of the education policy from the shortcoming of the system toward shortcomings in a proportion of the schools. One of the main assumptions behind the educational accountability system is that most schools are performing above average and system-wide reforms or action will not effectively address needs in particular schools that underperform. System-wide reforms that are initiated by the state level are not able to respond to the challenges encountered in the individual schools. Educational accountability policy is based on a belief in the single school and a mistrust of system-wide reform, because there are different challenges in different schools. Differences between schools act as the main argument against system-wide reforms and as an argument for output steering. When the policy documents fail to acknowledge that there are differences between schools, the policy that is envisaged loses its legitimacy.

So in the Norwegian education quality discourse, quality differences inside the system have not been an issue. This contrasts with many other education systems particularly that in the US, where the school one attends is regarded as crucial for individual outcome. Institutional confidence enters here, a well-researched tendency toward approval of public services in the Nordic countries. Differences in the quality of public services do not disrupt the strong public confidence in the welfare state's ability to distribute equal opportunities. Shortcomings are explained at the individual level and at the system level, but not by shortcomings at the organizational level. If the organization level isn't successful, this is held to be due to problems attributable to malfunctions at the state level or shortcomings at the individual level.

The groundwork documents convey an opposite position to that held in international educational accountability policy, i.e. the quality of the schools is high and there are no quality differences between schools. It is questionable if this position calls for the policy that the groundwork recommended.

9.1.4 Ineffective System – Money is not Enough

There is a clear transformation from the first reports from the *School Knows Best* project in 2001 to the Report to Stortinget *Culture for Learning* in 2004. The money is not enough approach that was the focus in the report from 2001 lost momentum during the period. The money is not enough argument is hardly visible in the report from 2004, but was one of the core arguments behind the development of educational accountability thinking in 2001. The reports from the *School Knows Best* reports outlined a clear economic and cost-effectiveness-related argument for educational accountability. The economic critique of the education system is related to the ineffective use of resources and a lack of systems or incentives to better mobilize existing resources (E. Hanushek & Raymond,

2001; Eric A. Hanushek, 2003; Eric Alan Hanushek & et al., 1994). Those issues had more or less disappeared by 2004.

When resources are not enough, what has to be added isn't clear, but a lack of incentives in the system may be the answer. In the *School Knows Best* reports, there was a clear assumption that the Norwegian school system did not have enough incentives for improvement, and external control systems and some form of free school choice were suggested. The Quality Committee did not follow this up and they saw incentives as a marketization of the education system, a pathway they strongly rejected. In the *School Knows Best* reports from 2002 and 2003, the lack of incentives was offered as a central explanation for the inefficacy of the system. Greater freedom of choice for parents between schools was discussed as a policy option that would motivate the schools to focus on objectives. Ultimately, though, ineffectiveness in schools was not used as a political argument to support the reform. The message was that the system is doing well, but ought to focus more on learning outcome.

9.2 Educational Accountability Policy

The policy discussed in the groundwork documents can be understood as a description of a new government approach rather than a new policy related to new objectives and functioning of the school system. All the documents emphasize the need for a more goal-oriented steering model and more freedom for individual schools or school districts. The policy follows international policy trends, i.e. the schools are to be given more freedom and are to be steered by measuring learning output. Schools are to be steered by making them responsible for their output, rather than by a policy that steers what goes on in school. The school content in itself is not an important issue in the new policy. Content is only a ground on which to learn basic skills. The school is no longer an agent in nation building, but a core institution for training the learning skills that are in demand.

Education accountability policy focuses on the responsibilities of the different levels in the education system and the school organization stands in the forefront as the main responsible unit. The school organization is only to a certain degree made responsible in the groundwork documents, but the system, i.e. the school owner, is considered to be the most responsible agent. In the end, it seems as if the schools do not know best after all. The municipality is the main accountable unit after all, even though the municipalities in Norway so far have only had a minor role in the education system as a technical facilitator for schools. A core assumption in international educational accountability policy, that schools are the accountable units, is downplayed in the policy documents. They do not establish a direct relation between the school and the public, but one between the public and the municipality. The Quality Committee emphasizes that the main responsible unit in the system is the school owner. The school owner, the political system in the municipality, is somehow equated with the public. It is the municipality that is to control and monitor the schools, and at the same time, to act as the main accountable unit. The municipalities are to reveal the output results, and at the same time, to be accountable for them. The students and parents are not given any particular role to control the schools by the Quality Committee.

9.2.1 From Input to Output

The traditional Norwegian input-centered education policy was questioned in all the groundwork documents. The shift from input to output also implies a shift in pedagogic approach. Instruction will have to be planned by first identifying the learning objectives rather than the learning content. This represents a didactic shift. Norway has a strong content-oriented learning plan tradition and learning method autonomy for teachers has been linked to how students work with content rather than learning methods as such. National learning plans have not stated what students were supposed to learn, but stated more what content students would encounter in school. In the White Papers from the Quality Committee, this shift of focus is also described as a didactic shift inside schools. Schools have been focusing too much on facilitating learning activities instead of focusing on the learning output of those activities. This is a criticism of input-oriented didactics with too little focus on the goals for instruction.

It isn't possible to identify a clear output steering model in the groundwork documents. There is a notion of more focus on output, but there are no clear models for output steering; there are rather discussions of consequences related to output or models for acting on information about the output. This resembles more of a didactic output model in which the learning plan and the instruction have to be goal-oriented. The old content and activity-orientated didactics are criticized and the groundwork documents convey an idea of an education system that has to be more goal-oriented.

9.2.2 From Professional Community to School Organization

Compared to international educational accountability policy, the school organization was not given any significant new role in the groundwork documents. There are no references to the development and measuring of school effect. International education policy attempts to control and manage the education system and the school organization has become the main address for the new steering policy, i.e. the political system controls the individual school. The new policy defines the school organization as the core unit for developing the education system. The policy breaks with traditional explanations of success or failure at the individual level, i.e. due to characteristics of teachers and students, toward an understanding of success or failure that depends on how the school as an organization is working. New educational accountability policies make an assumption that there is a correlation between the quality of the school as an organization and the quality of instruction in the classrooms. The school organization is to secure quality by management rather than by values and ethics developed in the professional community.

This steering model can threaten the power of the professional community. By establishing strong leadership at the organizational level and an important role for the school owner, the power of the professional community is challenged. The strong belief in quality steering by the ethics and morals developed in the self-regulated professional community is confronted by new models for steering. The school organization in modern education policy replaces the professional community by controlling and managing the teachers. The ethics and morals developed and embedded in the professional community are exchanged for organizational managing tools.

The international policy that targets the school organization as the unit that will secure quality is not visible in the documents. The shift toward school organization is not described. The pattern is the same, as the *School Knows Best* reports are more aligned with international policy in this respect too, and the succeeding documents try to adjust the policy to the Norwegian tradition. In Norway, it is the municipalities, or the local political system, that will control and manage the schools, and the role and the responsibilities of the schools are not clarified. The state level is only going to provide the information needed to make decisions at the local level. Small and weak political systems in the municipalities will bear the main burden of developing the schools based on the information the state level provides by testing output. The municipalities will have a new significant role and the state assumes that all municipalities will establish systems to control and manage their schools. The power of the professional teaching community is not really threatened by the small municipalities, but the large ones with their greater resources and capabilities may have the opportunity to develop a local policy that can give them power to steer the schools. The state level itself seems not to be prepared to challenge the power of the professional community.

9.3 Educational Accountability Tools

One of the most significant findings is that the political groundwork appears to be disconnected from international research and the development of accountability tools. Discussions targeting the distinct function of the tools and references to research on educational indicators are absent. According to the Quality Committee, the function of the tests is to gain information. The dynamic that the tools can put in play is rejected and a bulwark is established to avoid what was regarded as an unintended outcome of the policy tools. The policy ideas that accompany the tools are more or less absent or are rejected.

Though the results of the tests would be available to the public, they would not be presented in a way that would make it possible to rank schools, i.e. to compare the results. In this manner, Norwegian policy differed significantly from international policy. The centerpiece for accountability policy is the ranking of schools and the identification of failing schools. Identifying above average schools is not the point. The system's main function is to make quality differences between schools transparent for the public.

9.3.1 Student Achievement Tests

One of the main political issues since the OECD review of the Norwegian school system in 1989 had been the lack of a system to monitor the quality of the education system. The recommendations in the OECD review in 1989 did not suggest a system that created an accountability dynamic, but a monitoring system that made the state level able to develop a better input policy. Even if the review questioned the lack of accountability in the education system, it did not recommend a student test system that could make schools accountable for learning outcomes. It was first in the additional mandate for the Quality Committee (2002) that a clear political goal of establishing an achievement test-based accountability system was stated so that Norway could adopt a widely used and recommended policy. The policy was presented first in the *School Knows Best* reports, but during the political groundwork period, testing of students was absorbed into the external test system.

When the Quality Committee divided education quality into structure, process, and product quality, they suggested the establishment of a balanced accountability system. The aim was to divide responsibility between the state, municipality, and schools rather than to make the school responsible. Student achievement tests were not included to make schools accountable. Even though the Committee underlined that product quality was the most important indicator, the quality indicators chosen, relating to structure and process, the input, were beyond the control of the school organization. How the schools used resources or how they conducted the process wasn't part of the discussion.

The new additional mandate to the Quality Committee from the Ministry concluded that Norway would establish a national student test system, but did not define the function of tests. Even if the Ministry indicated that the committee should draw upon international experience with national student test systems, the mandate did not outline the function of such systems, stating only that Norway needed one.

In the transformation that educational accountability policy underwent, testing was the key issue. The *School Knows Best* project conveyed a clear definition of the purpose of the test system, i.e. to gain focus and mobilize existing resources. When the Quality Committee had finished its work, most known functions of a student test were embedded in the national test system. At the same time, the only reason for having a national test system was not stated, i.e. making schools accountable for the students' results in achievement tests. A weak test culture inside the education system might explain this confusion around the function of the national test system. In the US, there is a long tradition of testing inside the system. A new external test system would have to be justified as an addition to already existing tests. In a school system without a significant tradition of student testing, an external test was held to serve all kinds of purposes (Altrichter & Merki, 2010; Kühle & Peek, 2007). The unclear or the multiple functions of the test system would become a core issue in the implementation of the system.

The NQAS differed significantly from international education policy. When student tests set out to measure school quality, they have to be designed in a particular way. It is impossible to combine the diagnostic purposes of a student test and a student test that has the function of revealing the effect of the instruction. Norwegian exceptionalism might account for attempts to construct a multipurpose test system. Research on testing was not used to explore challenges in designing student tests that reveal school effect.

9.3.2 Identifying the Failing School Organizations

According to the political documents, failing schools do not exist in the Norwegian school system. The PISA report from 2001 supported this view and all the groundwork documents referred to the findings and conclusions in the national PISA report (Lie & Programme for International Student Assessment, 2001). In the light of what we know about all other Western countries, it is hard to understand that this view has not been challenged in Norway. That Norway does not have some schools that are systematically underachieving is almost hard to believe. What Lie concluded was that in the one-year PISA tests, there were greater differences inside schools than between schools. The conclusion is, and still is, that Norway does not have significant quality differences between schools. Educational accountability policy is to some extent a rejection of system-wide reforms and aims to create a policy that is directed at managing failing schools; it is also important that high-achieving schools are not distracted by reforms they do not need.

Quality differences between schools were not an issue in the political groundwork documents from 2001 to 2004. If we rely on the view that all schools in Norway have the same quality, there are no arguments supporting an implementation of an educational accountability system. There is no reason to make schools responsible or compare test results that are only explicable in terms of students' social background or intellectual endowment. The Norwegian accountability reform failed to establish a political understanding of the fact that educational opportunity for many students, mostly from low-income families and in rural areas, depends on the quality of the school they attend. Failing schools, and the organizational failure that explains that failure, is the main argument behind educational accountability. This argument was absent in the political groundwork documents. So Norwegian policy deviated from the trend in international education policy (Hirsch et al., 1995; OECD, 1998) toward a focus on the school as the responsible unit. External pressure on school organization was not seen in the Norwegian context as an appropriate way to develop the system, perhaps rather the opposite, being seen as something to avoid.

Education accountability policy sets out to narrow the achievement gap between schools. Some schools have pressure to achieve embedded in their local social environment. Others will need pressure to be exerted from the outside – often schools serving low-income families. These are no matters that the political groundwork dealt with since public services were assumed to always have the same quality, and differences in outcome were held to be due to the users. By defining the function of the student tests in a direction that didn't make schools "accountable" for the results in student achievement tests, the logic of an accountability system was absent. When the Committee pointed to the school owner as the responsible agent in the school system, they again redefined the system and so undermined the dynamic at the school level. The deep-rooted political belief in most Western countries that differences in school quality channel students from low-income families to low-performing schools is simply absent.

It is important to emphasize that the groundwork documents do not present the main political idea supporting educational accountability, i.e. the phenomenon of failing schools. The fact that Norway has not embraced the premises that are basic in international policy seems to be one of the main explanations for the limitations of Norwegian accountability policy. It seems to explain why Norway is running a NQAS without any distinct purpose. The political groundwork documents argue for a system, but at the same time, reveal a deficit of understanding in relation to what purpose the policy instruments are intended to serve. In the end, the tests inform the teachers about their own students. From being a tool in an output steering reform, testing took on the aspect of a state-imposed policy that mandated all teachers to test their students. As long as the main assumption is that there are no significant differences between schools, the policy documents struggle to establish a rationale for testing. The fact that there were (and are) differences in school output in Norway attributable to social background factors does not seem to have had any effect. The strong correlation between family background and school results would, in other Western countries, have been interpreted as a sign of low school effect, not as attributable to social class or ethnicity.

In the end, in the Report to Stortinget *Culture for Learning* in 2004, the national test system is suggested as a replacement for final examinations, revealing the extent of incomprehension about accountability and the role played by testing. However, this uncertainty about accountability has to be understood against a background of little public interest in quality differentiation in public services.

9.3.3 Decentralization

The recommendations in the OECD review in 1989 (OECD, 1989a) were not followed up, due to an endless debate about evaluation (Moe, 2010). However, they became relevant again after the PISA shock in 2001. Norway has had a strongly decentralized executive model for the education system, but a highly centralized steering model with regards to regulations and structure. In the modernization project *School Knows Best*, one of the five goals was to conduct a deregulation of the education system and to empower municipalities as school owners to make their own decisions based on local conditions. This would devolve powers from the state level but centralize the local management of schools. It was a decentralization of powers from the state level but a local centralization. The schools were supposed to be managed and run by the municipalities.

Norwegian central authorities (the ministry) seemed to expect the municipalities to make schools responsible. By providing information for the local political level, the state placed the responsibility of acting on it on the local level. For many decades, the state had a significant role in school development, entrusted to the state education offices in the 19 regions. This function was transferred to the municipalities, and the education offices would only conduct inspections related to the legal framework for schools. Decentralization of responsibility to the individual school is not a significant topic in the documents, it is more accurate to say that the role of the state is decentralized to municipalities and the school owners are given a larger role in the education system.

10. The Outcome: Differences and Similarities

Outcome refers to the result of a policy put into action. Comparing similarities and differences in outcome between the Norwegian reform and the common outcomes of educational accountability in other countries does not make sense since the policy implemented in Norway differs to such a large degree from international models that it is questionable if it is an educational accountability policy at all.

The reform of the national test system during the red-green coalition government removed all the features of the policy that could act as output controls. When the time for conducting the national test was moved (in 2006) to the beginning of the school year and the beginning of a school grade, the system could only survey the students and could not be used as an output steering tool.[6] Already in 2005, the Conservative coalition had lost support for national tests. Even the Liberal Party, a coalition partner, had a press release in February 2005 that claimed "… that the national test had to be moved to the beginning of the school year. The test was primarily intended to be guidance for the individual students' own learning."[7] It was not only the new red-green parties that wanted to move the test; the Liberal Party, which was part of the coalition, wanted to move the tests too, and described the main function of the national test system as the provision of information to the single student. This is a task that traditionally was entrusted to school tests and to teachers. Now the state intervened to inform the students about their challenges in connection with basic skills. The intended new output policy was turned into a strong input policy that intervened in the core business of schooling.

The strong correlation between social background and student achievement in the unified school system seemed to increase after the reform (Aasen, Karseth, & Møller, 2013).

---

6   It is interesting to note that one of the first political actions of the new social democratic government in Sweden conducted after eight years with the Conservative coalition was to move the national tests to the beginning of the school year.
7   Skei Grande, T. (2005). – Flytt de nasjonale prøvene [Press release]. Retrieved from http://www.nsd.uib.no/polsys/data/filer/parti/H8953.html.

10.1 The Municipal Accountability Policy

It might seem that accountability policy had failed in Norway, but this is only partly true. The accountability reform was also a decentralization reform and a re-establishment of the municipality as a school owner. The Norwegian school system was, before 1936, a municipal school system, where the single municipalities had control over their schools. Learning plans were decided at the municipal level. In 1936, a national learning plan was established by negotiation in parliament. So reform since 2000 has decentralized authority to municipalities that are more or less autonomous. Norway has over 420 municipalities with populations that range from 150 to 600,000, but all have the same responsibility to provide for public services such as schooling. Big municipalities have the capacity to develop their own education policy and are more or less disconnected from national policy. Most of the large municipalities in central areas have in fact developed their own educational accountability policy. Oslo has developed a sophisticated high-stake accountability system that uses some of the results from national tests as well as its own tests. When we compare educational accountability policies in Oslo, and municipalities in central areas of Norway, they are similar and do not differ much from international practice.

These practices are based on the notion that each school can attain results regardless of their students' family background and can convey the same expectations for all. School leaders can be discharged from their positions based on results and principals are hired based on outcome. But the many smaller municipalities in Norway do not have the capacity to develop and implement a local accountability policy. One of the outcomes of the reform is therefore a differentiated policy based on local capacity and a willingness to establish a local system for accountability at the school level.

10.2 The Geographic Achievement Gap

The geographic achievement gap in Norway is evident in the aggregated results from national tests. Again the issue of the geographic achievement gap has become an important political issue. The municipal school system is resulting in quality differences between rural and urban areas (Utdanningsspeilet 2012 : tall og analyse av grunnopplæringen i Norge, 2012). Oslo is the municipality in Norway where most emigrants to Norway settle, and despite the many low-income families in Oslo, the municipals have been ranked first in all quality indicators since 2006.

The school system until the late 1950s had learning plans for city schools and learning plans for rural schools. This can be compared with the division between Gymnasium and Hauptschule in central European tradition. The rural school did not give access to Gymnasium and further studies. The quality differences between schools in rural areas and urban areas were a central issue in national education policy after the Second World War. One of the most significant worldwide outcomes of educational accountability policy is the identification of a pool of schools, that despite yearly information on low performance, are not able to change practice and raise their instructional standards (Bidwell, Frank, & Quiroz, 1997; Mintrop, 2003, 2004a, 2004b; O'Day, 2005; Sadovnik et al., 2013). Low-performing schools are one of the main issues on the political agenda in states with a long tradition of educational accountability policy. The achievement gap increases between schools and school districts that are able to use information from the test system for development, and those that lack the capacity to use and benefit from the information, i.e. a pool of schools ends up in a deficit category (Faubert, 2009; OECD, 2011). The achievement gap between social groups is becoming more visible through a national accountability system for the public and the politicians. In the US, the achievement gap highlights the differences between social groups. The achievement gap that has developed in Norway is, however, not related to social differences, but to geographic location. Educational accountability requires capacity and competence that the small school districts seem to lack. The result is that the municipality-based accountability system created after 2005 has serious shortcomings.

The small municipalities see themselves as weak school owners or failing school owners and instruments to steer schools are only used to report on the results. Most school owners lack the capacity to connect to international education policy on their own, and they are dependent on support from the national level where in any case the political agenda is more than unclear. Schools don't seem to know best anymore and national policy is an input-based policy that most of the high-performing school districts seem to refuse and reject – or if adopted, is modified so as to be more output-oriented.

One of the main features of the Norwegian system is that it doesn't rank schools and so does not reveal failing schools. The quality of the service provided by the state is the same, except that students from low-income families don't succeed to the same degree as students from high-income families. There is a strong belief that variation in student achievement is found within schools and not between schools. The fact that low school quality or school effect actually strengthens the link between SES and performance in school is not reflected in Norwegian education policy.

Accountability systems that are based on student performance will necessarily rank the schools that serve low-income families and have low instructional quality at the bottom of the scale. Schools that serve middle-class students will have parents and after-school activities that can compensate for low instructional quality. Low-income families are dependent on high-quality instruction and how students perform in national tests is a result of learning in school. The lowest-ranked schools will be inner urban schools or schools serving first-generation immigrants. In the political discourse, an argument against ranking has been that it will stigmatize students from low-income families. But other schools serve the same student population and are able to bring their students above the average.

After years with an achievement-based accountability system, a pool of failing schools will emerge with the well-known combination of pupils drawn from low-income families aligned with low-quality instruction. The schools that are unable to change regardless of information given by the assessment system make the inequality of opportunity transparent and pose a political question. This hasn't happened in Norway. At the same time, schools that are serving middle-class students can perform around the average and schools that serve low-income families can score above the average. The accountability system isn't a ranking system with a clear bottom line.

There isn't any tradition in Norway for identifying unequal opportunities inside schools. There are no student categories such as "free-lunch students", "English learners", or "receiving support from child welfare services". This black-box understanding of student performance is also evident in OECD reports. In the review from 2011 of the Norwegian evaluation system, the authors claim:

> As in other Nordic countries, variations in student performance can mostly be found within schools. The between-school variation of performance in Norway is low by international standards, which indicates that the specific school a student attends has only a modest impact on how he or she performs (Nusche & OECD, 2011, p. 19).

The conclusion that schools in the Nordic countries only have a modest impact on student performance, compared with other parts of the world, seems to be a mantra that cements the Nordic-centric view. The belief that schools in Norway produce the same results will of course undermine any performance-based accountability system.

It is not possible for this study to conclude or to give a reliable description of the outcome of the educational accountability reform. One of the scholars engaged in the evaluation of the reform has asked if the schools did know best after all (Aasen, 2012).

"However, the purposes of the various tools and data sources established through NQAS have not been well communicated and there is little understanding of NQAS as a coherent system" (Nusche & OECD, 2011, p. 10).

A shift from an input- to an output-based policy will not be achieved in Norway as long as the output is not transparent. Pressure for control and transparency is often countered with the argument that a national test system is already established and supported by assertions about an overload of testing in the Norwegian school system.

10.3 Lack of Capacity

Because of the poor quality and extensive boycotting of the national tests, it is reasonable to conclude that attempts to implement a national educational accountability system failed. The Minister of Education Kristin Clemet said in 2008 that the implementation of the national tests under her leadership was so poor that coalition parties felt that they had no say when the new government started to reform the test system in 2005.

10.4 The State Level

The main function of the state level was to control and monitor the national education system by conducting national tests. The municipalities, as the school owners, were given responsibility to act based on the results.

When the state level is not able to monitor the system, the reform ends up as a decentralization reform where the municipal school system emerges. It seems as if Norway has reverted to a municipal school system where national institutions do not play any significant role. The municipal school system in Norway from 1880 to 1936 has in retrospect been viewed as a failure, and it was strongly criticized in its time.

The city municipalities are able to use national tests and additional local testing to control and manage the schools. In some senses, the state level seems to be irrelevant and the cities really connect to international education policy. The small municipalities, most of the school owners in Norway, do not have the capacity to use the system.

11. Conclusion – Convergence in Policy as Imitation

Norway has, of course, not been alone in the attempt to transfer a global education policy into a national context. Most OECD countries have implemented systems for evaluation and control of schools and national variation is considerable (Faubert, 2009). Convergence in education is occurring: policy is becoming more and more similar across national borders. Comparative education research has shifted from comparing national education systems based on different cultural and historical contexts to understanding schooling in the world society (R. Dale, 2005; Stefan Thomas Hopmann, 2008; Stefan T Hopmann, 2013; J. Spring, 2008). In the discourse on convergence in education policy, the case of Norway is an example of how a national context has transformed cross-national policy. Developments in Norway to some extent resemble cross-national trends, but in reality only some elements of international policy have been introduced. The output and outcome of the Norwegian accountability reform confirm the perception that international policy does not produce the same policy at the national level (Holzinger & Knill, 2005; Stefan Thomas Hopmann, 2003, 2008; Knill, 2005).

11.1 Education Policy as Imitation

Accountability is not part of the democratic discourse in Norway. As noted, the concept itself is non-existent in the Norwegian vocabulary. Making individuals accountable to the public is not part of Norwegian thinking about politics or public services. There is no debate around politicians' individual voting records. Political agreements are considered to be products of negotiation inside and between different political parties, interest organizations, and political institutions. A vote in parliament represents the end of long processes including different levels and organizations and is not usually understood as an expression of individual convictions or an individual's beliefs. The basic ideology behind educational accountability has been, and still is, absent in the Norwegian context.

There was no public pressure for educational accountability in Norway, and reasonably enough, this was not a feature of the groundwork for reform. If someone is accountable in the Norwegian context, it is not an organization but the profession that is held accountable, i.e. the teachers, the politicians, and the police, rather than the organization that produces the services. The strong professional communities stand in direct relation to the public. Education policy understood as control and steering challenges the power of the profession and Norwegian education policy has traditionally secured the position of the teachers rather than eroded it. Management tools at the organizational level can come into conflict with the fundamental belief in the autonomy of the professionals and their ability to define goals and evaluate.

The education quality discourse in Norway up to 2001 was rarely related to learning outcome at the school level. As described in Chapter 5, the education quality discourse that historically is embedded in the educational accountability tradition does not have any real counterpart in Norway. The strong input policy tradition in Norway has not led to a focus on student learning outcomes as an issue – these outcomes have been the responsibility of the professional community. In the policy discourse from 1945 to 2000, learning outcome has been more or less absent (Telhaug, 1999).

In the history of the development of educational accountability quality, differences between schools have had a decisive impact (Lessinger, 1970). The Norwegian accountability system was developed in a framework of perceived failure of the education system, i.e. the PISA shock, rather than the failure of particular schools. This mismatch between understanding of the problem and the policy tools that were imported created a unique national test system that is still running, i.e. a national testing system that does not have any distinct purpose (Nusche & OECD, 2011).

The Norwegian case does not fit into the scenario of a global epidemic of educational accountability policy. Norway has not adopted some kind of global neo-liberal education policy – where the state only facilitates a market for services. Seen from the outside, it may seem as if Norway is running a cross-national educational accountability policy, and even the OECD review in 2011 concluded that Norway has a NQAS (Nusche & OECD, 2011), but under the surface, the policy adopted differs significantly from cross-national models. In the evolution of educational accountability, the main political reflection or political conciseness behind the demand for accountability has been the assumption that unequal educational opportunities are products of differences in instructional quality between schools. School organizations are entrusted with the task of providing equal opportunities, so that achievement at school is not only to be determined by social background or talent. When Norway adopted a recommended model, the policy was not supported by the assumption of quality differences between schools. The groundwork documents did not convey any belief in the potential of the school as an organization. The policy followed the Coleman dictum – schools can't make any difference. The deep-rooted political beliefs that are embedded in educational accountability policy are not represented in Norwegian political culture. On the surface, the scenarios of the education system seem similar, the policy is similar, and the tools are similar, but still the output and the outcome are different.

It is not possible to describe the Norwegian policy of governing school as an accountability policy. The tools are in place, but they do not play any significant role in the national steering of the system. As we have seen, the Norwegian context did not have the bedrock of political beliefs and ideas that accountability rests on, and the political groundwork failed to establish these beliefs. One of the most important elements that might generate pressure for control and steering was absent, i.e. perceived shortcomings of the system.

In the case of Norway, it seems as if nations can share scenarios of the education system, but introducing policy instruments and tools that are deep-rooted in political beliefs is likely to fail. Adopting the same policy does not mean adopting the same political beliefs and ideas. P.A. Hall differentiates between policy paradigms and policy instruments and settings (Hall, 1993). The latter are more likely to change than the ideas and beliefs in a policy paradigm. A central question is whether it is possible to implement policy instruments, as tools for steering and control, when the fundamental ideas and beliefs behind the policy are absent. It is difficult to distinguish between a policy paradigm and a policy instrument; a policy instrument has to be developed and tuned to certain ideas or beliefs. When policy instruments and settings are transferred without the beliefs and ideas, the policy seems to be an imitation rather than an adoption. It is not likely to succeed in transferring a policy into a context where the political ideas and beliefs that are the basis for the policy do not exist. The political desire, as, for example, described in the additional mandate to the Quality Committee, to connect Norway to international education, is not the same as connecting with international political beliefs and ideas, but only to tools and practical policy. Nevertheless, a new policy has been developed in Norway that is more or less unknown in a global context, i.e. a highly expensive national test system that has the main function of informing teachers and students on the state of affairs at the individual level. The system is, in reality, part of an everyday practice in classrooms around the world, i.e. teachers are surveying the progress of their students. Public waste in Norway is often explained by the saying *because we can afford it*. The national economy makes Norway exceptional and a case that is difficult to generalize from, while most cultures have to legitimate the use of resources linked to a rational function and purpose.

A central question is whether policy was transformed. A transformation would imply the active and logical adjustment of a policy to some extent. But we have seen that the policy was not possible to comprehend in a Norwegian context. There does not seem to have been an active rejection of political beliefs or ideas, but the accountability paradigm was simply absent in the Norwegian context. There were no social or political groups that argued for more transparency at the school level. There were no issues about how the lack of quality threatened equal rights for education. There was no pressure for better distribution of education as a public good, etc. From a comparative perspective, the lack of public discourse and precision around quality differences between schools related to how they are able to secure and facilitate children's development of basic cultural/academic skills is difficult to convey and explain in an international context. Research in Norway that reveals quality differences at the school level is still understood as groundbreaking (Falch & Strøm, 2013), and is given little political and public attention. The main position in Norway is that there are not any significant quality differences between schools. The national tests and the practice of ranking schools is assumed to produce A and B schools. The logic is that the testing system produces the differences and not the quality differences in the classrooms. Ranking schools is understood as exposing students to public scrutiny, rather than the school. The centerpiece of the policy, the national assessment system, was not built around a political demand for transparency and accountability at the school level. The system is currently running, but the purpose and function of the system are still unclear (Nusche & OECD, 2011). It is therefore difficult to draw conclusions on what is the output and outcome of the reform. In 2012, the Ministry of Education conducted an evaluation of the system that was mostly focused on how teachers use and comprehend the information from the tests (Seland et al., 2013). The success of the system is assessed by the degree to which the tests can inform teachers about the skills of their own students. Parents were not viewed as a source for evaluating the system. The perspective in the evaluation reveals how the state level views the system. In the US and in other countries, it is expected that the teachers are constantly informing themselves through a variety of student tests, and that the state level is not conducting national tests to inform teachers. Teachers are using the results from the national tests at the student level to inform parents about the students' level of proficiency, not as information about the quality of the school or the teachers, but as an assessment of the quality of the students. Only a proportion of the parents are able to analyze the results and make sense of them by comparing their child's test score against the score of the school, municipality, and state. In this sense, the NQAS is adjusted to everyday life in mass schooling.

In comparative education research, great effort has been made and much research has been conducted to demonstrate the cross-national convergence in policy, while less effort has been given to revealing the convergence in education policy belief and ideas. It is possible to adopt a policy and at the same time reject the core beliefs and ideas behind the policy – not even actively reject the ideas and beliefs, but to transfer them to a new context as the same political history they fail to be understood or raised as a political issue. The Norwegian accountability reform is an example of how cross-national education policy seems to be similar, but also how the output and outcome are different to a degree that is it challenging to consider the policy as a sign of convergence in policy between states.

Norway was not able, despite the clear political objectives, to develop an educational accountability policy. The attempt to adopt the policy failed. The lack of knowledge, traditions, and capacity to build an accountability system became obvious during the development and implementation of the system. The numerous political attempts in the nineties to establish an external national quality system after the OECD review in 1989 had failed (Moe, 2010), and to some extent, the accountability reform suffered the same fate as earlier attempts to establish systems for quality control and monitoring.

The modernization project that was initiated by the new government in 2001 built on familiar conservative education policy thinking and a liberal approach to renewing the public sector – in our case, the education system. There was a clear link with international trends and the reports from the *School Knows Best* project (Norge . Utdannings- og forskningsdepartementet & Skolen vet best, 2002, 2003; Ødelien & Jacobsen, 2003) emphasized the lack of incentives and accountability in the education system. But some of the generic anxieties and preoccupations that have led to pressure for educational accountability systems seem to have been non-existent in the groundwork documents, i.e., failing schools, the achievement gap between social classes, the danger of disintegration or social exclusion, a public demand for transparency, etc. Argument and reflection, which are the bedrock for educational accountability systems that target the school level rather than the single student or single teacher, were not presented in the groundwork. The rationale for testing schools and making the results available to the public is not explicated in the core political documents. The Committee for Quality offered some explanations, but didn't establish a political platform or standpoint that an accountability policy could be built on.

Historically the expectation of equal learning outcome regardless of social background, gender, or race has been the bedrock argument for implementing systems that express a public pressure for educational quality for all. It is a public pressure for steering and control of the education system (Bobbitt, 1918a; Faubert, 2009; Lessinger, 1970; Linn, California Univ. Los Angeles. Center for the Study of Evaluation., & National Center for Research on Evaluation Standards and Student Testing Los Angeles CA., 2003; Mintrop & Trujillo, 2004). The political documents did not deal with the consequences of unequal opportunities or of quality differences between schools.

The equivocal signals from the Quality Committee subreport (Søgnen & Kvalitetsutvalget, 2002) that rejected and at the same time proposed an educational accountability system based on student achievement tests were an impossible compromise that made the subsequent process very difficult. During the political negotiations about the modernization project in parliament, i.e. the national test system, the Quality Committee reports, and *Culture for Learning*, the essential aim of national tests as a tool to create educational accountability was continually ignored. In 2004, the Education Committee in the Stortinget expressed its approval of the Ministry of Education's decision not to publish the test results, but argued all the same for quality control and quality monitoring at all levels in the system.[8] The political system seemed to lack fundamental understanding of the accountability system and most political parties, already in 2003, doubted the value of publishing results, but still argued strongly for output control by means of student testing.

Generic features and ideas behind educational accountability did not have, and still do not have, resonance in the Norwegian context. In contrast to the US, the school effect research tradition conveyed an optimistic view of what the school was able to accomplish, and willingness to take national action on the low-performing schools in the US was grounded in common interests among political parties (Mehta, 2013a). The accountability policy developed in Norway was inchoate, and if stated, it was rejected by most political parties. Single schools or school districts that underperform are still not a political issue in Norway, and the schools and districts concerned are not identified. Comparing schools and transparency as the centerpiece in the dynamics of educational accountability was unsettling from the beginning of the political

---

8   The other indicators proposed by the Quality Committee only reveal the amount of resources available in an already high-cost system, structure and process indicators that never had the power to explain any quality differences between schools.

process. The policy that transpired is more an imitation of a policy rather than a whole-hearted adoption of one.

11.2 The End of National Education Policy

Even though the educational accountability reform at the national level failed, school districts in the central areas of Norway during the reform developed and are now running sophisticated high-stake accountability systems. Despite the failure of the national system, the many school owners, who were made responsible by the reform, have developed an accountability policy at the local level. It is as if state education policy is not viewed as relevant for urban areas and that they have had to develop their own policy. In education, it is now possible for a school district to implement international policy, and the national level can reject the same policy. Education policy has been reduced to the management and control of a workforce.

The new national learning plan from 2006 that was developed in the wake of the accountability reform signifies in some ways the end of traditional national education policy. It is not possible to disagree with the platitudes in the learning plan. The plan in reality is a description of an adequate level of basic skills in the different grades – there are few if any political disagreements about the plan negotiated at the national level. In the area of national building, the schools were a key institution in the attempt to create a geographic collective by engagement in cultural and national myths. The national state ensured that everyone was exposed and was included in the myths. In the knowledge society, the political system at the state level no longer negotiates disagreements about the learning plan related to conflicting interests in nation building. It seems that the demands of the knowledge society define the objectives for schooling, i.e. the competence to learn. States are no longer running schools and education policy is reduced to management of a workforce in an institution – an exercise that politicians at the state level rather distance themselves from. Acting as a demanding employer for a strong group of voters seems to be a third rail for politicians on the national level. Politicians at the state level have transferred the governance of schooling to the local level and can without any obligations participate in the ongoing reflection within the teaching profession, rather than developing policy for steering and controlling the system. One result of the Norwegian accountability reform is that the steering of schooling is transferred to the local level and the school is adjusted to the capacity in the different municipalities. The state level only lends a supporting hand in connection with teacher training and initiatives that are more or less campaigns. The education system is often in comparative education analyzed at the state level and little research has been done on comparing education policy at the local or district level.

Education policy has to be analyzed as a flow of ideas at multiple levels: local, regional, international, etc. (Susan L Robertson, 2012). Policy is becoming a product in a constant state of innovation. This dynamic in current policymaking makes it possible for international organizations to serve as an arena for different actors and levels. International organizations are interesting as long as they provide the latest and newest in the innovation of scenarios and policy and are able to facilitate a meeting between different levels and agents. Political science that studies convergence in policy does not look at states as lenders or borrowers of policy, but studies how different levels are affected by policy, understood as output, and what the result is when the policy is implemented, understood as outcome.

11.3 Education Policy as Social Learning

Policymaking can be understood as a process of social learning (Hall, 1993; Heclo, 1974). The learning process develops more than policy instruments. It also generates and mediates fundamental ideas and beliefs that are embedded in these policy instruments. A policy is a result of a process of encountering challenges. The history of educational accountability policy development is a history of social and collective learning. Transferring the policy to a context that lacks the process of social learning that is behind the policy has to be considered as challenging. Accountability policy is not an idea collected from neo-liberal consultants or think tanks, but has evolved as a social learning process, in our case in the US context. That means, in facing social problems and shortcomings, that one has developed a policy over time and in a specific social setting. Educational accountability is part of the US education policy DNA and has developed over decades in an interaction between society and the state (Abelmann et al., 1999; R. F. Elmore, 1996, 1997, 2003; R. F. Elmore et al., 1994; R. F. Elmore et al., 1988; Fuhrman & Consortium for Policy Research in Education New Brunswick NJ., 1994; Mehta, 2013b). It has created deeply held beliefs and ideas in society that are embedded in the policy, i.e. regarding the function of schooling, social injustice between social and racial groups, the power distributed between the federal and state level, steering and control, etc. Educational accountability is a complex social contract between different stakeholders in the US (Mehta, 2013a, 2013b), a contract that is not so easy to adopt for new or different partners.

Even when the learning process behind the policy is lacking, ideas and policies have been disseminated in different settings and nations, and the learning process is a natural part of implementation, but the policy that is developed represents a different social learning process and the process will produce a new output and a new outcome (Almond & Verba, 1963).

Reflecting on the scenarios for education systems in the knowledge society, Norway was aligned with core international policy. Also, policy reflection was connected to international policy, how the school was going to be steered, the need for autonomy, from input to output steering, etc. A central question that arises is whether it is possible to identify a cross-national educational accountability policy. On the national level, it seems that there is evidence of this.

It is difficult to see the Norwegian accountability reform as a transformation process.

The social learning theory in comparative education gives the state a role, but at the same time, it understands policy as a result of social learning, and that it is not so easy to just adapt. Policymaking is a social learning process.

The Norwegian school system now more or less continues on the same path as before the accountability reform. The city municipality of Oslo had already started a system to make schools accountable before the national reform, and the accountability system in Oslo is disconnected with the national system, and runs on its own, independently of education policy at the national level.

11.4 The Lost Logic

After the failure in implementing the system, the effort to reform it under the red-green government from 2005 to 2009 aimed to keep the framework of a NQAS, but at the same time, the policy removed all the accountability dynamic. From the outside, it might seem as if Norway is running an educational accountability system, but the system lacks the structure and content essential to make schools responsible (Nusche & OECD, 2011). The output steering policy that was introduced by the *School Knows Best* project and the Quality Committee was, during the red-green government in 2005–2013, replaced by a clear input policy (Norge. Kunnskapsdepartementet, 2006, 2008), i.e. the government re-established the state level as an agent for development at the school level by the use of regulations and input policy. Educational accountability became a school district matter. The term "national" is no longer used by the Directorate for Education and Training. As has been shown, it is questionable to consider the system in place as an educational accountability system. It isn't understood as one, but has much of the same structure and tends to be connected to international trends. Even the current Minister of Education, Torbjørn Røe Isaksen from the Conservative Party, takes the view that it isn't possible or meaningful to compare the results of national tests between school districts.[9] Norwegian education policy discourse is in this case disconnected from international trends. In a UK or US context, a politician that thinks it isn't meaningful to compare results between schools due to geographic differences, social class, or race would have had to explain why expectations are differentiated. Alternatively, explain why it is accepted that some students are served by low-performing schools, and not least, what politicians are going to do to fix failing schools. Consequences for low-income families that are often served by low-performing schools were not problematized, nor was the issue of how low-income families suffer from low school effect. Differences in school performance are not used as an argument for demanding transparency and educational accountability to monitor and secure equal opportunities. Reflection on school effect was not part of the political groundwork, i.e. why students in school B are doing better than those in school A, and what the consequences are. It seems like the differences between the continental learning plan tradition and the Anglo-American tradition of autonomy and control (Haft & Hopmann, 1990; S. Hopmann, 1991; S. Hopmann et al., 1998; Isaksen, 2008) materialize when educational accountability is implemented in a continental learning plan context. In the Norwegian context, there has been an antithesis between evaluation as control and evaluation for development (Haug, 2009; Roald, 2010). In the Anglo-American context, an educational accountability system has been viewed as both, i.e. control and development are not considered to be contradictions. Pedagogical values as an argument for the implementation of national testing might have been a selling argument, but when the system was developed and put into action, the pedagogical motive was in the foreground, deployed to convert the policy to the use of an internal diagnostic system that was aligned with common practice in school. In the end, the logic of the system was reduced to informing teachers about their own students. The political criticism of the education system after the PISA shock in 2001 was aimed at the school system, not at the school level. Understanding learning output as an organizational product instead of as a result of individual achievements at the student and teacher level is a foundation for an accountability system. The Norwegian accountability policy lacked this bedrock premise for an accountability system at the school level. The main assumption that the accountability system is created to identify the low-performing schools and that the low-performing schools have to respond

---

9   Røe Isaksen, T. (2013). Mer åpenhet om nasjonale prøver [Press release]. Retrieved from https://www.regjeringen.no/no/aktuelt/-mer-apenhet-om-nasjonale-prover/id744713/.

was not articulated in the policy behind the national test system. National testing was again evaluated in 2012 on the initiative of the Ministry of Education. It was the pedagogical values of the system that were evaluated, not the accountability dimension. Teachers were asked if the system gave adequate information about their students (Seland et al., 2013).

11.5 Comparative Education and National Culture

A crucial omission in the processes that set out to reframe school policy after 2000 was a focus on quality differences between schools. Government was perhaps badly advised in this connection, since at that time, it could easily have been shown that these significant differences were present. There seems to have been a collective failure to recognize the importance of this issue within the educational establishment irrespective of whether the actors were trade unionists, representatives of interest organizations, academics, educational administrators, or politicians. Underperforming schools were never put on the agenda. This led to a kind of socially constructed silence around the key issue within the entire accountability discourse. This silence of course has its historical resonances, since educational research and the teaching profession have been so closely linked in Norway throughout the post-Second World War epoch. Development in education has been a professional monopoly for the teaching profession and education researchers, an enclave in which discussion of inequality of opportunity and its causes and consequences has been scarcely admissible. The documentation we have examined shows that the content of international policy, with its emphasis on the school as the arena where social differentiation or discrimination can be offset, was not embedded in the reform process. Social equality concerns were filtered out. Opposition to testing and ranking could draw upon skepticism about radical departures in school policy, determined professional opposition and a kind of shallow populism playing upon fears of stigmatization. But much more effective was a kind of reflex assumption that gross social inequalities, inherent in the functioning of a central social institution such as school could not occur in Norway with its equitable and democratic political traditions and an ethos of public services that enjoys widespread support and approval.

By focusing on the social and economic forces behind education reforms and policy, comparative education can overlook how ideas and beliefs in a national context exert a powerful influence and can frustrate efforts at innovation. Traditionally changes in education systems have been linked to developments in philosophical or pedagogical ideas. Differences in value systems and ideology play a significant role in the development of education policy. Social and economic conditions can encourage development, but values and cultural contexts at the national level can scarcely be ignored.

The paradox of the accountability reform process as it unfolded in Norway is that social and geographical inequalities in student performance will in all likelihood persist in the foreseeable future, lending credibility to the view that the Liberal transformation that has affected the whole of society in recent decades has its costs in the form of social exclusion and marginalization. One vantage point on this scenario is that it has been precisely the rejection of newer directions and rationales in Liberal policy that set out to reform the school by rendering it responsible to its users, by introducing transparency and user participation, that has brought this about.

Bibliography

Aasen, P. (1999). Det sosialdemokratiske prosjektet – Utdanningsreformer i Svergie og Norge i etterkrigstiden. In A. O. Telhaug & P. Aasen (Eds.), *Både – og 90-tallets utdanningsreformer i historisk perspektiv.* Trondheim/Oslo: Cappelen.

Aasen, P. (2012). *Kunnskapsløftet som styringsreform – et løft eller et løfte? : forvaltningsnivåenes og institusjonenes rolle i implementeringen av reformen.* Oslo: NIFU.

Aasen, P., Karseth, B., & Møller, J. (2013). *Reformtakter : om fornyelse og stabilitet i grunnopplæringen.* Oslo: Universitetsforl.

Aasen, P., & Telhaug, A. O. (1999). *Både – og : 90-tallets utdanningsreformer i historisk perspektiv.* Oslo: Cappelen akademisk forl.

Abelmann, C., Elmore, R., Even, J., Kenyon, S., Marshall, J., & Consortium for Policy Research in Education Philadelphia PA. (1999). *When Accountability Knocks, Will Anyone Answer?* (CPRE-RR-42). Retrieved from Pennsylvania: http://www.cpre.org/Publications/rr42.pdf

Adick, C. (2005). Transnationalisierung als Herausforderung für die international und interkulturell vergleichende Erziehungswissenschaft. *Tertium comparationis, 11*(2), 243–269.

Almond, G. A., & Verba, S. (1963). *The civic culture : political attitudes and democracy in five nations.* Princeton, N.J.: Princeton university press.

Altrichter, H., & Merki, K. M. (2010). *Handbuch Neue Steuerung im Schulsystem:* Springer.

Amos, K. (2010). Governança e governamentalidade: relação e relevância de dois conceitos científico-sociais proeminentes na educação comparada. *Educação e Pesquisa, 36,* 23–38.

Amrein, A. L., & Berliner, D. C. (2002). High-Stakes Testing & Student Learning. *Education Policy Analysis Archives, v10 n18 Mar 2002.*

Apple, M. W. (2000). Creating profits by creating failurse: standards, markets, and inequality in education. *International Journal of Inclusive Education, 5*(2/3), 103–118.

Apple, M. W. (2001). *Educating the "right" way : markets, standards, God, and inequality.* New York ; London: RoutledgeFalmer.

Arbeids- og administrasjonsdepartementet. (2002). *Fra ord til handling : redegjørelse om modernisering, effektivisering og forenkling i offentlig sektor.* Oslo: AAD.

Arnove, R. F. (1980). Comparative Education and World-Systems Analysis. *Comparative Education Review, 24*(1), 48–62. doi:10.2307/1187395.

Bailey, S. K., & Mosher, E. K. (1968). *ESEA; the Office of Education administers a law* ([1st ed. ed.). Syracuse, N.Y.]: Syracuse University Press.

Ball, S. J. (1993). What is policy? Texts, trajectories and toolboxes. *The Australian Journal of Education Studies, 13*(2), 10–17.

Ball, S. J. (1998). Big Policies/Small World: An Introduction to International Perspectives in Education Policy. *Comparative education, 34*(2), 119–130. doi:10.2307/3099796.

Ball, S. J. (2000). *Sociology of education : major themes.* London: Routledge.

Bartlett, W., & Le Grand, J. (1993). *Quasi-markets and social policy.* Basingstoke: Macmillan Press.

Bauer, S. C. (2000). Should Achievement Tests Be Used To Judge School Quality? *Education Policy Analysis Archives, v8 n46 2000.*

Behn, R. D. (2001). *Rethinking democratic accountability.* Washington, D.C.: Brookings Institution Press.

Bell, D. (1973). *The coming of post-industrial society a venture in social forecasting.* New York: Basic Books.

Berg, G. (1983). Developing the Teaching Profession: Autonomy, Professional Code, Knowledge Base. *Australian Journal of Education, 27*(2), 173–186.

Berg, G. (1995). *Skolkultur – nyckeln till skolans utveckling : en bok för skolutvecklare om skolans styrning.* Göteborg: Förlagshuset Gothia.

Bergesen, H. O. (2006). *Kampen om kunnskapsskolen*: Universitetsforlaget Oslo.

Berliner, D. (2005). Our Impoverished View of Educational Reform. *Teacher College Record.*

Bernstein, B. (1973). *Class, codes and control* (2nd ed.). London: Routledge & Kegan Paul.

Bernstein, B., & Centre for Educational Research and Innovation. (1975). *Class and pedagogies : visible and invisible.* Paris,.

Bidwell, C. E., Frank, K. A., & Quiroz, P. A. (1997). Teacher Types, Workplace Controls, and the Organization of Schools. *Sociology of Education, 70*(4), 285–307.

Bieber, T., & Martens, K. (2011). The OECD PISA study as a soft power in education? Lessons from Switzerland and the US. *European Journal of Education, 46*(1), 101–116.

Biesta, G. J. (2004). Education, accountability, and the ethical demand: Can the democratic potential of accountability be regained? *Educational Theory, 54*(3), 233–250.

Biesta, G. J. J. (2004). Education, Accountability, and the Ethical Demand: Can the Democratic Potential of Accountability Be Regained? *Educational Theory, 54*(3), 233–250.

Biesta, G. J. J. (2005). Against learning. Reclaiming a language for education in an age of learning. *Nordisk Pedagogik, 25*(1), 54–66.

Bobbitt, J. F. (1918a). *The curriculum.* Boston, New York: Houghton Mifflin Company.

Bobbitt, J. F. (1918b). The Plan of Measuring Educational Efficiency in Bay City. *The Elementary School Journal, 18*(5), 343–356. doi:10.2307/993733.

Bobbitt, J. F. (1924). *How to make a curriculum.* Boston, New York Houghton Mifflin company.

Bobbitt, J. F. (1941). *The curriculum of modern education* (1st ed.). New York,: McGraw-Hill Book Company, inc.

Bowles, S., & Levin, H. M. (1968). The Determinants of Scholastic Achievement-An Appraisal of Some Recent Evidence. *The Journal of Human Resources, 3*(1), 3–24. doi:10.2307/144645.

Bryk, A. S., & Schneider, B. L. (2002). *Trust in schools : a core resource for improvement.* New York: Russell Sage Foundation.

Bunda, M. A. (1979). Accountability and Evaluation. *Theory into Practice, 18*(5), 357–362. doi:10.2307/1476753.

Carnoy, M., Elmore, R. F., & Siskin, L. S. (2003). *The new accountability : high schools and high-stakes testing.* New York: RoutledgeFalmer.

Chubb, J. E., & Moe, T. M. (1990). *Politics, markets, and America's schools.* Washington, D.C.: Brookings Institution.

Clemet, K. (2002). Additional mandate [Press release]

Clemet, K. (2008, 07.23.) *Clemet gir seg selv strykkarakter på nasjonale prøver/Interviewer: NTB.* Verdens Gang, VG, Oslo.

Codd, J. A. (1988). The construction and deconstruction of educational policy documents. *Journal of Education Policy, 3*(3), 235–247.

Coleman, J. S., Hoffer, T., & Kilgore, S. (1982). *High school achievement : public, Catholic, and private schools compared.* New York: Basic Books.

Coleman, J. S., National Center for Educational Statistics, & Forente stater . Department of Health Education and Welfare. (1966). *Equality of educational opportunity.* Washington: U.S. Departement of Health, Educationm, and Welfare.

Crossley, M. (2000). Bridging Cultures and Traditions in the Reconceptualisation of Comparative and International Education. *Comparative education, 36*(3), 319–332. doi:10.1080/713656615.

Dale, E. L. (1975). *Til kamp mot funksjonærpedagogikken : foredrag.*

Dale, E. L. (1980). *Hva er oppdragelse? : en studie i sosialpedagogikk.* Oslo: Gyldendal.

Dale, E. L. (1986). *Oppdragelse, ideologikritikk og pedagogikk.* Oslo: Universitetsforlaget.

Dale, E. L., & Wærness, J. I. (2002). *Eksamen og læring - nasjonal strategi for vurdering og kvalitetsutvikling.* Retrieved from Oslo: http://www.laeringslaben. no/images/files/1Underveisrapport1.pdf.

Dale, R. (2000). Globalization and Education: Demonstrating a "Common World Educational Culture" or Locating a "Globally Structured Educational Agenda"? *Educational Theory, 50*(4), 427–448.

Dale, R. (2005). Globalisation, Knowledge Economy and Comparative Education. *Comparative education, 41*(2), 117–149. doi:10.2307/30044528.

Dale, R., & Robertson, S. L. (2009). *Globalisation and europeanisation in education.* Oxford, U.K.: Symposium Books.

Dalin, P. (1982). *Skoleutvikling.* Oslo: Universitetsforlaget.

Dalin, P., & Rust, V. D. (1983). *Can schools learn?* Windsor: Nfer-Nelson.

Dent, M., Bagley, C., & O'Neill, M. (1999). *Professions : new public management and the european welfare state.* Staffordshire: Staffordshire University Press.

Diamond, J. B. (2012). Accountability policy, school organization, and classroom practice: Partial recoupling and educational opportunity. *Education and Urban Society,* 0013124511431569.

Diamond, J. B., Spillane, J. P., & Northwestern Univ. Evanston IL. Inst. for Policy Research. (2002). *High Stakes Accountability in Urban Elementary Schools: Challenging or Reproducing Inequality? Institute for Policy Research Working Paper* (IPR-WP-02–22). Retrieved from Illinois:

Djelic, M.-L., & Sahlin-Andersson, K. (2006). *Transnational Governance Institutional Dynamics of Regulation.* Cambridge: Cambridge University Press.

Drezner, D. W. (2001). Globalization and Policy Convergence. *International Studies Review, 3*(1), 53–78. doi:10.1111/1521-9488.00225.

Drucker, P. F. (1969). *The age of discontinuity : guidelines to our changing society.* New York: Harper & Row.

Drucker, P. F. (1993). *Post-capitalist society.* Oxford: Butterworth-Heinemann.

Earl, L., Nusche, D., Maxwell, W., & Shewbridge, C. (2011). *OECD Reviews of Evaluation and Assessment in Education: Norway 2011.* Paris: OECD Publishing.

Edmonds, R. (1979). Effective Schools for the Urban Poor. *Educational Leadership, 37*(1), 15–18,20–24.

Edvardsen, E. (1977). *Småsamfunnets sosialiserings-potensiale.* Tromsø: <E. Edvardsen>.

Edvardsen, E. (1984). *Den gjenstridige allmue : (skole og levebrød i et nordnorsk kystsamfunn ca. 1850-1900).* Tromsø: [E. Edvardsen].

Edvardsen, E., & Universitetet i Tromsø. (1985). *Å føye sammen det atskilte.* Tromsø: [E. Edvardsen].

Ekholm, M., & Ploug Olsen, T. (1991). *Förbättringar av skolor : nordiska lärdomar och internationell inspiration inför 2000-talet.* København: Nordisk ministerråd.

Elmore, R. (2003). Accountability and Capacity. In M. Carnoy, R. Elmore, & L. S. Siskin (Eds.), *The new accountability : high schools and high-stakes testing.* New York: RoutledgeFalmer.

Elmore, R., & Fuhrman, S. H. (2001). Holding Schools Accountable: Is it working? *Phi Delta Kappan, 83*(1), 67–70,72.

Elmore, R. F. (1996). Getting to Scale with Good Educational Practice. *Harvard Educational Review, 66*(1), 1–26.

Elmore, R. F. (1997). The Politics of Education Reform. *Issues in Science and Technology, 14*(1), 41–49.

Elmore, R. F. (2003). The challenges of accountability. *Educational Leadership, 61*(3), 6–10.

Elmore, R. F., Abelmann, C. H., & Fuhrman, S. H. (1996). The New Accountability in state Education Reform: From Process to Performance. In H. F. Ladd (Ed.), *Holding schools accountable.* Washington D.C.: Brookings Institution.

Elmore, R. F., & Center for Policy Research in Education. (1990). *Restructuring schools : the next generation of educational reform* (1st ed.). San Francisco: Jossey-Bass.

Elmore, R. F., Fuhrman, S., & Association for Supervision and Curriculum Development. (1994). *The governance of curriculum.* Alexandria, Va.: The Association.

Elmore, R. F., McLaughlin, M. W., National Institute of Education (U.S.), & Rand Corporation. (1988). *Steady work : policy, practice, and the reform of American education.* Santa Monica, CA.: Rand Corp.

Elstad, E., Hopmann, S., Langfeldt, G., & Achieving School Accountability in Practice. (2008). *Ansvarlighet i skolen : politiske spørsmål og pedagogiske svar : resultater fra forskningsprosjektet "Achieving School Accountability in Practice".* [Oslo]: Cappelen akademisk forl.

Engeland, Ø., Roald, K., & Langfeldt, G. (2008). *Kommunalt handlingsrom : hvordan forholder norske kommuner seg til ansvarsstyring i skolen?*

Esping-Andersen, G. (1990). *The three worlds of welfare capitalism* (Vol. 6): Polity press Cambridge.

Esping- Andersen, G. (1989). The three political economies of the welfare state. *Canadian review of sociology/Revue canadienne de sociologie, 26*(1), 10–36.

Evetts, J. (2009). New professionalism and new public management: Changes, continuities and consequences. *Comparative Sociology, 8*(2), 247–266.

Falch, T., & Strøm, B. (2013). Kvalitetsforskjell mellom videregående skoler? *Tidsskrift for samfunnsforskning, 5404,* S. 437–462.

Faubert, V. (2009). School evaluation: Current practices in OECD countries and a literature review.

Fend, H. (1984). *Die Pädagogik des Neokonservatismus* (1. Aufl. ed.). Frankfurt am Main: Suhrkamp.

Forente stater. National Commission on Excellence in Education, & USA Research (Firm). (1984). *A nation at risk : the full account.* Portland,Or.: USA Research.

Frønes, I. (2010). *Kunnskapssamfunn, sosialisering og sårbarhet.*

Frønes, I., & Strømme, H. (2010). *Risiko og marginalisering : norske barns levekår i kunnskapssamfunnet.* Oslo: Gyldendal akademisk.

Fuchs, T., & Wossmann, L. (2003). *What Accounts for International Differences in Student Performance? A re-examination using PISA Data.* Retrieved from Munchen:

Fuhrman, S., & Consortium for Policy Research in Education New Brunswick NJ. (1994). *Politics and Systemic Education Reform. CPRE Policy Briefs.* Retrieved from New Jersey.

Gadamer, H.-G. (1965). *Wahrheit und methode : Grundzüge einer philosophischen Hermeneutik* (2. Aufl. ed.). Tübingen: Mohr.

Gadamer, H.-G. (1967). *Das Problem der Sprache.* Mynchen.

Giroux, H. A. (2005). The terror of neoliberalism: Rethinking the significance of cultural politics. *College Literature, 32*(1), 1–19.

Goodlad, J. I. (1977). An Ecological Approach to Change in Elementary-School Settings. *The Elementary School Journal, 78*(2), 95–105. doi:10.2307/1001332.

Gordon, L., & Whitty, G. (1997). Giving the 'Hidden Hand' a Helping Hand? The Rhetoric and Reality of Neo-Liberal Education Reform in England and New Zealand. *Comparative Education, v33 n3 p453–67 Nov 1997, 33*(3), 453–467.

Granheim, M., Lundgren, U. P., & Tiller, T. (1990). *Utdanningskvalitet – styrbar eller ustyrlig? : om målstyring og kvalitetsvurdering av norsk skole.* Oslo: TANO.

Granheim, M. K., & Lundgren, U. P. (1990). *Steering by goals and evaluation in Norwegian education.* Oslo: Norges råd for anvendt samfunnsforskning.

Grendstad, G., Selle, P., Bortne, Ø., & Strømsnes, K. (2006). *Unique environmentalism : a comparative perspective.* New York: Springer.

Grimen, H. (2005). Profesjonsetikken sitt grunnlag. *Nyhetsbrev, 3.*

Haft, H., & Hopmann, S. (1990). *Case studies in curriculum administration history.* London: Falmer Press.

Hall, P. A. (1993). Policy paradigms, social learning, and the state: the case of economic policymaking in Britain. *Comparative politics,* 275–296.

Hanushek, E., & Raymond, M. E. (2001). The Confusing World of Educational Accountability. *National Tax Journal, 54*(2), 365–384.

Hanushek, E. A. (2003). The Failure of Input-Based Schooling Policies. *Economic Journal, 113*(485), F64-F98.

Hanushek, E. A., & et al. (1994). *Making Schools Work: Improving Performance and Controlling Costs.* District of Columbia: Brookings Institution, 1775 Massachusetts Avenue, N.W., Washington, DC 20036 Brookings Institution, Washington, DC.

Hanushek, E. A., & Kimko, D. D. (2000). Schooling, labor force quality, and the growth of nations.. *American Economic Review, 90,* 1184–1208.

Haug, P. (2009). *Kvalitet i skulen og internasjonal påverknad.*

Heclo, H. (1974). Social policy in Britain and Sweden. *New Haven.*

Helgesen, M. (2000). *Nye former for demokratisk deltakelse : borgere, brukere og kunder i skolen.* Bergen: LOS-senteret.

Hellesnes, J. (1975). *Sosialisering og teknokratiein sosialfilosofisk studie med særleg vekt på pedagogikkens problem.* Oslo ,: Gyldendal.

Hellesnes, J. (1976). *Socialisering og teknokrati.* København: Gyldendal.

Hellesnes, J., Dale, E. L., Strømnes, Å. L., Polarstjerna, Studentersamfunnet i Tromsø, & Landslaget for norske lærerstudenter. (1975). *Pedagog eller funksjonær.* Oslo: Novus.

Hernes, G., & Knudsen, K. (1976). *Utdanning og ulikhet.* Oslo: Universitetsforl.

Hirsch, D., St. John-Brooks, C., OECD, & Centre for Educational Research and Innovation. (1995). *Schools under scrutiny.* Paris: OECD.

Hoëm, A. (1969). *Skolen og heimen.*

Hoëm, A. (1978). *Sosialisering / en teoretisk og empirisk modellutvikling.* Oslo ,: Universitetsforlaget.

Holzinger, K., & Knill, C. (2005). Causes and conditions of cross-national policy convergence. *Journal of European public policy, 12*(5), 775–796.

Hopman, S. T. (2007). *PISA zufolge PISA : hält PISA, was es verspricht?* Wien: LIT.

Hopmann, S. (1991, April 3–7). *The Multiple Realities of Curriculum Policy Making*. Paper presented at the Annual Meeting of the American Educational Research Association, Chicago IL.

Hopmann, S., Gundem, B. B., & Universitetet i Oslo . Pedagogisk forskningsinstitutt. (1998). *Didaktik and/or curriculum : an international dialogue*. New York: P. Lang.

Hopmann, S., & Kunzli, R. (1997). Close Our Schools! Against Current Trends in Policy Making, Educational Theory, and Curriculum Studies. *Journal of Curriculum Studies, 29*(3), 259–266.

Hopmann, S. T. (2003). On the evaluation of curriculum reforms. *Journal of Curriculum Studies, 35*(4), 459–478.

Hopmann, S. T. (2008). No Child, No School, No State Left behind: Schooling in the Age of Accountability. *Journal of Curriculum Studies, 40*(4), 417–456.

Hopmann, S. T. (2013). The end of schooling as we know it? *Journal of Curriculum Studies, 45*(1), 1–3.

Høgmo, A., & Solstad, K. J. (1977). *The Lofoten project : towards a relevant education*. [Tromsø]: University of Tromsø, Department for Social Science.

Høgmo, A., Tiller, T., Solstad, K. J., & Lofotprosjektet. (1981). *Skolen og den lokale utfordring : en sluttrapport fra Lofotprosjektet*. Tromsø : Universitetet i Tromsø.

Ingersoll, R. M. (1997). *Teacher Professionalization and Teacher Commitment: A Multilevel Analysis. Statistical Analysis Report* (ED406349). Retrieved from

Isaksen, L. S. (2002). *Utdifferensieringen av den norske skole : norsk skole i et systemteoretisk perspektiv*. [Trondheim]: L.S. Isaksen.

Isaksen, L. S. (2008). Skoler i gapestokken. In E. Elstad, S. Hopmann, & G. Langfeldt (Eds.), *Ansvarlighet i skolen : politiske spørsmål og pedagogiske svar : resultater fra forskningsprosjektet "Achieving School Accountability in Practice"* (pp. S. 271–291). Oslo: Cappelen akademisk forl.

Jakobi, A. P., & Martens, K. (2010). *Mechanisms of OECD governance international incentives for national policy-making?* Oxford: Oxford University Press.

Jeffrey, J. R. (1978). *Education for children of the poor : a study of the origins and implementation of the Elementary and Secondary Education Act of 1965*. Columbus, Ohio: Ohio State University Press.

Kahlenberg, R. D. (2001). Learning from James Coleman. *Public Interest*(144), 54–72.

Kamens, D. H., & Benavot, A. (2011). National, regional and international learning assessments: trends among developing countries, 1960–2009. *Globalisation, societies and education, 9*(2), 285–300.

Kandel, I. L. (1933). *Comparative education*. Boston: Houghton Mifflin.

Kirke- utdannings- og forskningsdepartementet. (1991). *Om organisering og styring i utdanningssektoren : St.meld. nr. 37 (1990–91)*. [Oslo]: Departementet.

Kirke- utdannings- og forskningsdepartementet. (1992). *Kunnskap og kyndighet : om visse sider ved videregående opplæring*. Oslo: Departementet.

Knill, C. (2005). Introduction: Cross-national policy convergence: concepts, approaches and explanatory factors. *Journal of European Public Policy, 12*(5), 764–774.

Koehl, R. (1977). The Comparative Study of Education: Prescription and Practice. *Comparative Education Review, 21*(2/3), 177–194. doi:10.2307/1187656.

Kogan, M., Granheim, M., & Lundgren, U. P. (1990). *Evaluation as policymaking : introducing evaluation into a national decentralised educational system*. London: Jessica Kingsley Publishers.

Kristvik, E. (1920). *Folkelagnad : tankar om samfund og kultur*. Kristiania: Norli.

Kühle, B., & Peek, R. (2007). Lernstandserhebungen in Nordrhein-Westfalen. Evaluationsbefunde zur Rezeption und zum Umgang mit Ergebnisrückmeldungen in Schulen. *Empirische Pädagogik, 21*(4), 428–447.

Ladd, H. F. (1996). *Holding schools accountable : performance-based reform in education*. Washington, D.C.: Brookings Institution.

Langfeldt, G. (2011). *Ansvarsstyrning – didaktikens slutpunkt?*

Le Grand, J. (2001). *The Quasi-market Experiments in Public Service Delivery: Did it work?* Paper presented at the Pontignano.

Le Grand, J., & University of Bristol. School for Advanced Urban Studdies. (1990). *Quasi-markets and social policy*. Bristol: School for advanced urban studies, University of Bristol.

Lessinger, L. M. (1970). *Every kid a winner : accountability in education*. New York: Simon and Schuster.

Lessinger, L. M. (1971). Educational Engineering: Managing Change to Secure Stipulated Results for Disadvantaged Children. *The Journal of Negro Education, 40*(3), 277–281. doi:10.2307/2966512.

Lessinger, L. M., & Sabine, C. D. (1973). *Accountability: systems planning in education*. [Homewood, Ill.]: ETC Publications.

Lessinger, L. M., & Tyler, R. W. (1971). *Accountability in education*. Worthington, Ohio,: C. A. Jones Pub. Co.

Levin, B. (1998). An Epidemic of Education Policy: (what) can we learn from each other? *Comparative education, 34*(2), 131–141. doi:10.1080/03050069828234.

Levin, H. M. (1974). A conceptual framework for accountability in education. *The School Review*, 363–391.

Levitt, T. (1986). *Marketing Imagination: New*: Simon and Schuster.

Lie, S., Caspersen, M., & Björnsson, J. K. (2004). *Nasjonale prøver på prøve; Rapport fra en utvalgsundersøkelse for å analysere og vurdere kvaliteten på oppgaver og resultater til nasjonale prøver våren 2004*. Retrieved from Oslo:

Lie, S., & Programme for International Student Assessment. (2001). *Godt rustet for framtida? : norske 15-åringers kompetanse i lesing og realfag i et internasjonalt perspektiv*. [Oslo]: Institutt for lærerutdanning og skoleutvikling, Universitetet i Oslo.

Linn, R. L., California Univ. Los Angeles. Center for the Study of Evaluation., & National Center for Research on Evaluation Standards and Student Testing Los Angeles CA. (2003). *Accountability: Responsibility and Reasonable Expectations. CSE Report* (CSE-R-601). Retrieved from California:

Luhmann, N. (1997). Globalization or world society: how to conceive of modern society? *International Review of Sociology, 7*(1), 67–79.

Luhmann, N., & Schorr, K.-E. (1979). *Reflexionsprobleme im Erziehungssystem*. Stuttgart: Klett-Cotta.

Lundahl, L. (2002). Sweden: Decentralization, Deregulation, Quasi-Markets-And Then What? *Journal of Education Policy, 17*(6), 687–697.

Lundgren, U. (1990). Oecd-rapporten – en bakgrunn. In M. Granheim, U. P. Lundgren, & T. Tiller (Eds.), *Utdanningskvalitet – styrbar eller ustyrlig? : om målstyring og kvalitetsvurdering av norsk skole* (pp. 411). Oslo: Tano.

Lundgren, U. P. (1979). Educational Evaluation: A Basis for, or a Legitimation of, Educational Policy. *Scandinavian Journal of Educational Research., 23*(2), 31.

Lundgren, U. P. (2011). PISA as a political instrument *Pisa Under Examination* (pp. 17–30): Springer.

Martin Carnoy, & Diana Rhoten. (2002). What Does Globalization Mean for Educational Change? A Comparative Approach. *Comparative Education Review, 46*(1), 1–9. doi:10.1086/324053.

McEwen, N. (1995). Introduction: Accountability in Education in Canada. *Canadian Journal of Education / Revue canadienne de l'éducation, 20*(1), 1–17. doi:10.2307/1495048.

McWalters, P., & Cheek, D. W. (2000). A State Accountability System as a Technology of Social Control: The Case of Rhode Island, USA. *Evaluation and Research in Education, 14*(3&4), 268–276.

Mehta, J. (2013a). *The allure of order : high hopes, dashed expectations, and the troubled quest to remake American schooling*. Oxford: Oxford University Press.

Mehta, J. (2013b). How Paradigms Create Politics The Transformation of American Educational Policy, 1980–2001. *American educational research journal*, 0002831212471417.

Merkle, J. A. (1980). *Management and ideology: The legacy of the international scientific management movement*: Univ of California Press.

Meyer, J. W., & Krücken, G. (2005). *Weltkultur: wie die westlichen Prinzipien die Welt durchdringen*: Suhrkamp.

Midtsundstad, J. H., & Hopmann, S. (2011). *Didaktiske posisjoner i et nordisk perspektiv*.

Mintrop, H. (2003). The Limits of Sanctions in Low-Performing Schools: A Study of Maryland and Kentucky Schools on Probation. *Education Policy Analysis Archives, v11 n3 2003*.

Mintrop, H. (2004a). High-Stakes Accountability, State Oversight, and Educational Equity. *Teachers College Rec, 106*(11), 2128–2145.

Mintrop, H. (2004b). *Schools on probation : how accountability works (and doesn't work)*. New York: Teachers College Press.

Mintrop, H., & Trujillo, T. (2004). *Corrective Action in Low-Performing Schools: Lessons for NCLB Implementation from State and District Strategies in First-Generation Accountability systems*. Retrieved from Los Angeles:

Moe, O. (2010). Ulike sider ved elevvurdering – noen prinsipielle betraktninger. *Bedre skole*(1), 28–34.

Morgan, C. (2006). Transnational governance: The case of the OECD PISA. *polity*, 202.

Mortimore, P. (2004). *Equity in education : thematic review*. Paris: OECD.

Mundy, K. (1998). Educational multilateralism and world (dis) order. *Comparative education review, 42*(4), 448–478.

Murnane, R. J., & Raizen, S. A. (1988). *Improving Indicators of the Quality of Science and Mathematics Education in Grades K-12*: ERIC.

Måsvær, L. (2005, December 9.). – Nasjonale prøver styrker opplæringa. *Forkning.no*. Retrieved from http://www.forskning.no/artikler/2005/desember/1133783704.82.

Nir, A. E. (2003). Quasi-Market: The Changing Context of Schooling. *International Journal of Educational Reform, 12*(1), 26–39.

Norge. Kirke- og undervisningsdepartementet. (1987). *Mønsterplan for grunnskolen : M87* (Bokmål[utg.] ed.). Oslo: Kirke- og undervisningsdepartementet : Aschehoug.

Norge. Kirke- utdannings- og forskningsdepartementet. (1992). *Kunnskap og kyndighet : om visse sider ved videregående opplæring*. Oslo: Departementet.

Norge. Kirke- utdannings- og forskningsdepartementet. (1996). *Om elevvurdering, skolebasert vurdering og nasjonalt vurderingssystem.* [Oslo]: [KUF].

Norge. Kirke- utdannings- og forskningsdepartementet. (1999). *Mot rikare mål : om einskapsskolen, det likeverdige opplæringstilbodet og ein nasjonal strategi for vurdering og kvalitetsutvikling i grunnskolen og den vidaregåande opplæringa.* [Oslo]: Departementet.

Norge. Kunnskapsdepartementet. (2006). *-og ingen sto igjen : tidlig innsats for livslang læring.* [Oslo]: Departementet.

Norge. Kunnskapsdepartementet. (2008). *Kvalitet i skolen.* Oslo: Departementet.

Norge. Utdannings- og forskningsdepartementet. (2003). *Om ressurssituasjonen i grunnopplæringen m.m St.Meld. nr 33 (2002-2003)* (pp. 69 s.).

Norge. Utdannings- og forskningsdepartementet. (2004). *Culture for Learning.* [Oslo]: Departementet.

Norge. Utdannings- og forskningsdepartementet, & Skolen vet best. (2002). *Skolen vet best : situasjonsbeskrivelse av norsk grunnopplæring : november 2002.* Oslo: Utdannings- og forskningsdepartementet.

Norge. Utdannings- og forskningsdepartementet, & Skolen vet best. (2003). *Situasjonsbeskrivelse av norsk grunnopplæringen : juni 2003.* Oslo: Utdannings- og forskningsdepartementet.

Norge. Utdannings- og forskningsdepartementet, & The Situation in Primary and Secondary Education in Norway. (2003). *The Situation in Primary and Secondary Education in Norway* Oslo: Utdannings- og forskningsdepartementet.

Norge. Utdannings- og forskningsdepartementet, K. f. l. (2004). *Kultur for læring.* (St.meld ;). [Oslo]: Departementet.

Nusche, D., & OECD. (2011). *OECD reviews of evaluation and assessment in education : Norway 2011.* [Paris]: OECD.

O'Day, J. (2005). Standard-based reform and low-performing schools. In F. M. Hess (Ed.), *Urban school reform: Lessons from San Diego* (pp. 115–138). Cambridge, Mass.: Harvard Education Press.

O'Neill, O. (2002a). *Autonomy and trust in bioethics*: Cambridge University Press.

O'Neill, O. (2002b). *A question of trust.* Cambridge: Cambridge University Press.

Oakes, J. (1989). What educational indicators? The case for assessing the school context. *Educational Evaluation and Policy Analysis, 11*(2), 181–199.

OECD. (1976). *OECD-vurdering av norsk utdanningsvesen : OECD-eksaminatorens rapport.* [Oslo]: Aschehoug.

OECD. (1987). *Reviews of national policies for education: Norway.* Retrieved from Paris:

OECD. (1989a). *OECD-vurdering av norsk utdanningspolitikk : norsk rapport til OECD : ekspertvurdering fra OECD*. Oslo: Aschehoug.

OECD. (1989b). *Reviews of national policies for education: Norway*. Retrieved from Paris:

OECD. (1995). *Governance in transition : public management reforms in OECD countries*. Paris: OECD.

OECD. (1996). *The knowledge-based economy*. Paris: Organisation for Economic Co-operation and Development.

OECD. (1998). *Overcoming failure at school*. Paris: OECD.

OECD. (2001a). *The Well-being of nations : the role of human and social capital*: OECD.

OECD. (2001b). *What Schools for the Future?* : OECD Publishing.

OECD. (2011). How are schools held accountable? *Education at a Glance 2011: OECD Indicator* (pp. 429–449): OECD.

Ogawa, R., Collom, E., & California Educational Research Cooperative Riverside. (1998). *Educational Indicators: What Are They? How Can Schools and School Districts Use Them?* Retrieved from California:

Olssen, M. (2006). Understanding the mechanisms of neoliberal control: lifelong learning, flexibility and knowledge capitalism. *International Journal of Lifelong Education, 25*(3), 213–230.

Olssen, M., Codd, J. A., & O'Neill, A.-M. (2004). *Education policy: Globalization, citizenship and democracy*: Sage.

Olssen*, M., & Peters, M. A. (2005). Neoliberalism, higher education and the knowledge economy: from the free market to knowledge capitalism. *Journal of Education Policy, 20*(3), 313–345.

Parsons, T. (1966). *Societies : evolutionary and comparative perspectives*. Englewoood Cliffs, N.J.: Prentice-Hall.

Power, M. (1994). *The audit explosion*. London: Demos.

Power, M. (1997). *The audit society : rituals of verification*. Oxford: Oxford University Press.

Power, M. (2003). Auditing and the production of legitimacy. *Accounting, organization and society, 28*, 379–394.

Power, M. (2004). Counting, control and calculation: Reflections on measuring and management. *Human Relation, 57*(6), 765–783.

Rattsø, J. (2001). Det er ikke penger som er problemet i norsk skole. *Horisont*(3), 10–20.

Regjeringserklæringen. (2005). *Plattform for regjeringssamarbeidet mellom Arbeiderpartiet, Sosialistisk Venstreparti og Senterpartiet, av 20. desember 2005. (Soria Moria Erklæringen).* Retrieved from http://www.regjeringen.no/up load/SMK/Vedlegg/2005/regjeringsplatform_SoriaMoria.pdf.

Rinne, R., Kallo, J., & Hokka, S. (2004). Too Eager to Comply? OECD Education Policies and the Finnish Response. *European Educational Research Journal,* 3(2), 454–485.

Roald, K. (2010). *Kvalitetsvurdering som organisasjonslæring mellom skole og skoleeigar.* Psykologisk fakultet, Universitetet i Bergen, [Bergen].

Robertson, S. L. (2005). Re-Imagining and Rescripting the Future of Education: Global Knowledge Economy Discourses and the Challenge to Education Systems. *Comparative education,* 41(2), 151–170. doi:10.2307/30044529.

Robertson, S. L. (2012). Signposts in 'doing'critical transnational educational policy analysis.

Robertson*, S. L. (2005). Re- imagining and rescripting the future of education: global knowledge economy discourses and the challenge to education systems. *Comparative education,* 41(2), 151–170. doi:10.1080/03050060500150922.

Rosenau, J. N., & Czempiel, E.-O. (1992). *Governance without Government Order and Change in World Politics.* Cambridge: Cambridge University Press.

Rosenmund, M. (2000). OP-ED Approaches to international comparative research on curricula and curriculum-making processes. *Journal of curriculum studies,* 32(5), 599–606.

Rosenmund, M. (2007). The current discourse on curriculum change: A comparative analysis of national reports on education *School knowledge in comparative and historical perspective* (pp. 173–194): Springer.

Rothstein, R. (2004). Class and schools: Using social, economic, and educational reform to close the achievement gap. *Washington, DC: Economic Policy Institute.*

Sadovnik, A. R., O'Day, J. A., Bohrnstedt, G. W., & Borman, K. M. (2013). *No Child Left Behind and the reduction of the achievement gap: Sociological perspectives on federal educational policy:* Routledge.

Sciara, F. J., & Jantz, R. K. (1972). *Accountability in American education.* Boston,: Allyn and Bacon.

Seland, I., Vibe, N., & Hovdhaugen, E. (2013). *Evaluering av nasjonale prøver som system* (Vol. 2013/4). Oslo: NIFU.

Sethne, A. (1917). *Efterligning og aktivitet hos barn.*

Sethne, A. (1953). *Normalplanene av 1939 : en merkepel i norsk skole.*

Sethne, A., & Killingstad, A. (1928). *Hjemstedslære : håndbok for lærere*. Oslo: Cappelen.

Silverman, H. J., & Gadamer, H.-G. (1991). *Gadamer and hermeneutics*. New York: Routledge.

Skirbekk, G., & Heidegger, M. (1999). *Dei filosofiske vilkår for sanning : ei tolking av Martin Heideggers sanningslære* (2. utg. ed.). Bergen: Filosofisk institutt, Universitetet i Bergen.

Solstad, K. J. (1965). *Utkantungdom og flytting*. Oslo: K.J. Solstad.

Solstad, K. J. (1984). *Ein skole for samfunnet*. [Oslo]: Cappelen.

Solstad, K. J. (1988). *Ein samfunnsaktiv skole : korfor – kva – korleis*: Skoledirektøren i Nordland.

Spranger, E. (1928). *Kultur und Erziehung : gesammelte pädagogische Aufsätze* (4. verm. Aufl. ed.). Leipzig: Quelle & Meyer.

Spranger, E. (1932). *Volk, Staat, Erziehung : Gesammelte Reden und Aufsætze*. Leipzig.

Spring, J. (2008). Research on globalization and education. *Review of Educational Research, 78*(2), 330–363.

Spring, J. H. (2005). *The American school, 1642–2004* (6th ed.). Boston: McGraw-Hill.

Stark, M. (1998). No Slow Fixes Either: How Failing Schools in England are Being Restores to Health. In L. Stoll & K. Myers (Eds.), *No quick fixes : perspectives on schools in difficulty*. London ; Washington, D.C.: Falmer Press.

Stromquist, N. P. (2000). Editorial. *Compare: A Journal of Comparative and International Education, 30*(3), 261–264. doi:10.1080/713657475.

Søgnen, A., & Kvalitetsutvalget. (2002). *Førsteklasses fra første klasse : forslag til rammeverk for et nasjonalt kvalitetsvurderingssystem av norsk grunnopplæring : delutredning fra et utvalg oppnevnt ved kgl. res. 5. oktober 2001 : avgitt til Utdannings- og forskningsdepartementet 14. juni 2002*. Oslo: Statens forvaltningstjeneste, Informasjonsforvaltning.

Søgnen, A., & Kvalitetsutvalget. (2003). *I første rekke : forsterket kvalitet i en grunnopplæring for alle*. Oslo: Statens forvaltningstjeneste, Informasjonsforvaltning.

Søgnen, A., Kvalitetsutvalget, & Utdannings- og forskningsdepartementet. (2002). *Førsteklasses fra første klasse : forslag til rammeverk for et nasjonalt kvalitetsvurderingssystem av norsk grunnopplæring*. Oslo: Statens forvaltningstjeneste, Informasjonsforvaltning.

Tangerud, H. (1980). *Mønsterplanen i søkelyset*. Oslo: Universitetsforlaget.

Taylor, F. W. (1911). *The Principles of scientific management*. New York: Harper & Brothers.

Telhaug, A. O. (1990). *Den nye utdanningspolitiske retorikken : bilder av internasjonal skoleutvikling*. Oslo: Universitetsforl.

Telhaug, A. O. (1992). *Norsk og internasjonal skoleutvikling : studier i 1980-årenes restaurative bevegelse*. [Oslo]: Ad Notam Gyldendal.

Telhaug, A. O. (1999). *Norsk utdanningspolitisk retorikk 1945-2000 : en studie av utdanningstenkningen i norske partiprogrammer*. [Oslo]: Cappelen akademisk forl.

Tenorth, H.-E. (1994). *Alle alles zu lehren Möglichkeiten und Perspektiven allgemeiner Bildung*. Darmstadt: Wissenschaftliche Buchgesellschaft.

Tenorth, H.-E. (2004). Bildungsstandards und Kerncurriculum. *Zeitschrift für Pädagogik*(5), 650–661.

Thelen, K. (1999). Historical institutionalism in comparative politics. *Annual review of political science, 2*(1), 369–404.

Thrupp, M. (1998). Exploring the Politics of Blame: School Inspection and Its Contestation in New Zealand and England. *Comparative education, 34*(2), 195–209.

Thuen, H., & Vaage, S. (2004). *Pedagogiske profiler : norsk utdanningstenkning fra Holberg til Hernes*. Oslo: Abstrakt forl.

Tiller, T. (1975). *Organisering av undervisning med lokalt og regionalt stofftilfang : erfaringer fra "Lofotprosjektet"*. Tromsø,.

Tiller, T. (1979). *Samfunnsorientert undervisning – en alternativ basis for undervisningsorganisering*. [Trondheim]: [T. Tiller].

Tiller, T. (1980). *Samfunnsorientert undervisning, pedagogisk fornyelsesarbeid og lærerkompetanse*. [Tromsø]: Universitetet i Tromsø, [Inst.for samfunnsvitenskap].

Tiller, T., & Tiller, R. (2002). *Den andre dagen : det nye læringsrommet*. Kristiansand: Høyskoleforl.

TNS-Gallup. (2004). *Rektorers og læreres erfaringer med de nasjonale prøvene 2004*. Retrieved from Oslo: http://www.udir.no/Upload/Rapporter/5/Evaluering_av_de_nasjonale_provene_2004.pdf?epslanguage=no.

Travers, K. J., & Westbury, I. (1989). *The IEA study of mathematics I: Analysis of mathematics curricula*. Elmsford, NY, US: Pergamon Press.

Turmo, A., Lie, S., Ibsen, E., & Hopfenbeck, T. N. (2005). *Nasjonale prøver på ny prøve : rapport fra en utvalgsundersøkelse for å analysere og vurdere kvaliteten på oppgaver og resultater til nasjonale prøver våren 2005 Acta didactica 1/2005*

Tyack, D. B., & Cuban, L. (1995). *Tinkering toward utopia a century of public school reform.* Cambridge, MA: Harvard University Press.

Tyler, R. W. (1971). Accountability in perspective. In L. M. Lessinger & R. W. Tyler (Eds.), *Accountability in Education* (pp. 1–4). Worthington, Ohio: C. A. Jones Pub. Co.

Undervisningsdepartementet, K. o. (1987). [Mønsterplan for grunnskolen : M 87].

United States. National Commission on Excellence in Education. (1983). *A nation at risk : the imperative for educational reform : a report to the Nation and the Secretary of Education, United States Department of Education.* Washington, D.C.: The Commission : for sale by the Superintendant of Documents, U.S. Government Printing Office.

Universitets- og høyskoleutvalget, & Hernes, G. (1988). *Med viten og vilje : innstilling fra Universitets- og høyskoleutvalget oppnevnt ved kongelig resolusjon av 22. juli 1987 : avgitt til Kultur- og vitenskapsdepartementet 9. september 1988.* Oslo ,: Forvaltningstjenesten.

Utdanningsspeilet 2012 : tall og analyse av grunnopplæringen i Norge. (2012). Oslo: Utdanningsdirektoratet.

Wagner, R. B. (1989). *Accountability in education : a philosophical inquiry.* New York ; London: Routledge.

Walford, G. (1996). School Choice and the Quasi-market in England and Wales. *Oxford studies in comparative education, 6*(1).

Weiss, M., & Steinert, B. (1996). Germany: competitive inequality in educational quasi-markets. *Oxford studies in comparative education, 6*(1).

West, A., Noden, P., Edge, A., & David, M. (1998). Parental Involvement in Education in and out of School. *British Educational Research Journal, 24*(4), 461–484.

West, A., & Pennell, H. (2000). Publishing School Examination Results in England: Incentives and Consequences. *Educational Studies, 26*(4), 423–436.

Ødelien, S., & Jacobsen, G. (2003). *Evaluering av "Skolen vet best" : Utdannings- og forskningsdepartementets prosjekt for bedret finansiering, organisering, kvalitetsvurdering og administrasjon av grunnopplæringen.* Oslo: Statskonsult.

Østerud, P., & Johnsen, J. (2003). *Leve skolen! : enhetsskolen i et kulturkritisk perspektiv.* Vallset: Oplandske bokforl.

Ålvik, T. (1991). *Skolebasert vurdering : en innføring.* Oslo: Ad notam.

www.ingramcontent.com/pod-product-compliance
Lightning Source LLC
LaVergne TN
LVHW050142060326
832904LV00004B/137